"Barry has really dug deep to share his own personal sales journey and identity crisis around how to successfully serve in a sales role while not resorting to unethical or manipulative practices. This book is inspirational and instructive for a LOT of people out there struggling to improve or find clarity in their sales career. Barry has really identified a pain point and a common uncomfortable task that we all face as business people. Finding balance to sell passionately but not over do it to appear like the, "Sleezy salesperson" - can be challenging."

Dale Archdekin
Founder at Smart Inside Sales

"The way Barry shares his experiences through his failures and successes has helped him continue to be relatable, trustworthy and an authority figure in sales and the real estate industry for over 20 + years. "Too Nice for Sales" is a must-read and must share - hands down."

Daryl Towe
Co-founder CTAB

Too Nice for Sales

Too Nice for Sales

A Practical Guide to Ethical Lead Conversion

Barry Jenkins, Jr.

XULON PRESS

Xulon Press
2301 Lucien Way #415
Maitland, FL 32751
407.339.4217
www.xulonpress.com

Paperback ISBN-13: 978-1-66283-532-2
Ebook ISBN-13: 978-1-66283-533-9

DEDICATION

THIS BOOK IS dedicated to my wife, Nicole. I wanted to hire someone to write this book for me. In her gentle and unique way, she strongly encouraged me to write this book myself. For this, I am very grateful! In every area of my life, she's made me a better man by just being in my life. Nicole, thank you for loving me, for supporting me, and making all of my dreams come true. I love you!

TABLE OF CONTENTS

Foreword
by Tristan Ahumada

I MET BARRY Jenkins through a popular Facebook group that focuses around exploring the science of Real Estate. He stood out because the value he was always giving was on point and very useful. It took 3 years for me to meet him in person and when I did I didn't realize he was 6'6", *"this dude is tall"*, was my first thought. We later met up again at different events and one time at an event in DC he drove up from his hometown of Virginia Beach to meet me and talk tech. It was Barry, Juefeng Ge (Co-Founder of Ylopo), and I. Barry was going to drive us to a small mastermind at someone's house. Barry missed the off ramp 2 times and we went in a 20 minute circle trying to get back in the right direction all while we talked about technology and what books we should be reading next. It was a very cool time we spent in the car together. One note to the reader though, if you ever find yourself in the car with Barry, be sure that you don't talk to him and distract him because he will miss his exit!

I've known Barry Jenkins for about 6 years now and the one thing that stands about him over everything else is his *kindness*. His approach to every situation, personal or business, is one of sincere understanding. His stoic demeanor is refreshing in a business world where people tell you to buy this or that and almost force their opinions on you. I believe that the world we live in has pivoted over the last few years into a place where you, as a salesperson, will be able to connect deeper and stand out among the crowd the more genuine and sincere your approach is.

This is why I love this book. It's one that you don't normally see written by successful agents. It's the opposite of being loud and in your face and it all starts with listening to those you want to attract. Barry's genius lies in breaking down the process of connecting with any client through a journey. He leads you through a path that rewards you with a complete understanding of what it takes to succeed in Real Estate in the current era we work in.

You'll love the fact that Barry doesn't just outline what you should do in theory, this is all tested and practical. He not only writes it all out, he continually practices this for himself and with his team!

You better believe I shared this with all my agents, my teams, my brokerage, and those I teach. It's a book you will go back to often because you will use it as a manual for real estate sales. ***Enjoy***!

Introduction:
How This Book Came
to Fruition

I'm NOT REALLY a person my friends and family thought would ever write a book. Nothing about my growing up said, "This kid's going to be an author one day." It could have been my C and D averages in English, the fact that I didn't know what a noun was defined as until my wife taught me in my twenties, or the fact that I didn't read books regularly until I was in my early twenties. My childhood was made up of playing sports and having fun. I had zero to no interest in anything academic. I've been told this has helped my writing style be a tad more conversational in tone since I haven't been formally trained. Which is a nice way of saying I have a limited vocabulary. Regardless, I run one of the top real estate teams in America and I am a person who has a story to tell. I felt this story would be best told via a small book.

This book, *Too Nice for Sales*, is a compilation of moments from my life and what those moments in each chapter taught me about sales. I have been in the real estate business for more than twenty years now and have had several life events that caused me to look at the industry a tad differently than others. My current team sells 850+ homes a year and we are the #1 largest team in the state of Virginia according to a recent *RealTrends* report. We sell a lot! In 2012 I sold 125 homes by myself without any staff or administration working for me. From 2011 through 2021, I've always had an abundance of sales. I feel very strongly that the market crash of 2008–2010 provided me with several opportunities to learn how to be successful in the following decade. Unsurprisingly, tremendous suffering taught me a lot about life, business, and how to make something out of nothing.

It was by being broke and working in other industries part-time to survive that I learned many new skills regarding how to make selling real estate the success it is for me today. These approaches have not only caused my team to rise in success but have caught the attention of the founders of the highly successful and innovative digital marketing firm Ylopo. Over the course of five years, I've gone from an occasional consultant to a full-time executive with a dual focus on product and training while running my real estate team. In this executive role, I was given the unique honor of being in charge of the content and direction of the training for new Ylopo users. Much of the principles found in this book were formalized while teaching Ylopo users how to be successful.

Finally, being exposed to the rawness and tricks found in the sales industry allowed me to have a crisis of my faith. I have several degrees, with two of them being in theology and ministry. I also was a pastor of a church for ten years. While this book is not focused on my faith in Jesus Christ and the Bible, that faith is most certainly a foundation of much of what you will learn in the following pages. I say this because I was forced to find a way to be successful while still attempting to follow my understanding of what's correct in the Bible.

Many times I was being taught somewhat shady tactics to make a sale by my employer, and with the pressure of having to provide for my family, it proved to be very difficult for me. By God's grace, I was able to find creative and insightful methods to remain upright and ethical while still using engaging approaches to sell a product. This really has become the foundation of my book.

What's interesting is that there are numerous events in the Bible that required followers of God to challenge their thinking to succeed in the tasks before them. For example, Paul on Athen's Hill talking about an unknown God versus starting out talking about Jesus, Daniel having to eat a vegetarian meal in Babylon to avoid meat given to idols, and when Jesus taught about the shrewd servant who was fired and how sinners are more shrewd with money than His followers. Each of these examples required someone who was attempting to do the right thing in a way that didn't fit the usual mold. While this book will by no means shove my faith in Jesus down your throat, I want to be candid with you, the reader, that I was able to create a sales approach by attempting to stay true to my faith. Amazing things can happen when we stand up for what we believe in!

My hope for you is that you are able to internalize much of what is shared in the following pages so that you too can be motivated to do the right thing, for the right reasons, and be wildly successful as you do so. There is absolutely no reason you have to degrade yourself to lying, cheating, and stealing to have a successful business. Further, I believe authenticity sells more than anything else in our culture today. When you represent yourself as an authentic human, people will feel it and be compelled to refer you business and purchase your products.

Last, please make sure you review the action items at the end of each chapter. I added these because I may at times get caught up in a book I am enjoying, and I forget to take actionable takeaways that immediately impact my business. Rather than just enjoy this book, I want you to have something to implement after each short chapter. I have also created a course to help you execute on this book that you can find on toonicefor-sales.com . You'll benefit greatly from this approach!

It is my sincere desire that you benefit from these concepts as much as I have!

PART ONE

1.

How to View an Opportunity

I was selling shoes and bussing tables when my first opportunity in real estate arrived. At the time, I was fresh out of high school and working from ten a.m. to nine p.m., six days a week. I worked so much I didn't have time to spend my money. But all that changed one day when my stepdad approached me with an opportunity.

His offer was this: I could buy a house with cash, in my name, and a lender would even finance the work that needed to be done to the house. The only catch? I had to sell the house within a year, or refinance it, because the investor wanted his money back in twelve months.

I did what any other eighteen-year-old would do. I took my chances and bought the house. It was scary but exciting—and for the first time in my young adult life, it felt like there were no limits to all of these possibilities that were ahead of me! Twelve months later (just when I thought things couldn't get crazier), I sold this property as well as made more than $20,000 off it—more than double what either one of my then-current jobs could make me in a six-month period. I was hooked. And so from then on out, every year or two, I bought a house or two—with each flip making just enough money to keep going until the next purchase, and I never looked back.

After my second flip, I decided to get a real estate license. My stepmom and dad were also getting into the business, so now my entire family was in the game. It made sense because from 2002 to 2007, homes sold quickly, with financing being free-flowing and there being virtually no safeguards against home prices inflating too much. Of course, this was before 2008, when everything crashed. But as someone who had been a broke twenty-year-old, 2002 to 2007 felt like a golden age for my business.

I thought I had it all, but then reality smacked me in the face and made sure to remind me that life isn't always easy.

From 2008 to 2010, closings started to fall apart... regularly. Suddenly I went from selling homes in minutes to not selling anything. Banks weren't equipped to navigate the short sale process, and millions of dollars in sales went up in smoke. I remember praying in my little two-bedroom house for God to answer my prayer and please send me business. The ads we ran in magazines weren't working. Online lead generation wasn't really on the radar yet, and I hadn't bothered to keep any kind of database of past clients to stay in contact with. I had nothing but my phone, and that wasn't ringing either.

It wasn't long before my wife and I began to feel the weight of more than $50,000 of credit card debt. Without the comfortable income real estate had provided, we were forced to use our credit cards for simple things such as groceries and gas. Eventually the cards were all maxed out and no one would extend any more credit to me due to having so many lines of credit tapped out. I started to seriously consider filing for bankruptcy.

It was during this environment of debt and confusion that several other problems began to arise, likely a result of my stress levels. My appendix began leaking and I was misdiagnosed by my doctor, so it leaked for another twenty-four hours. The next day I was in so much pain that we went to the ER. A month and two rounds of surgery later, I was finally home. My exhausted seven-months-pregnant wife had to carry the load of her job, my health, our home, and everything in between.

Just when it seemed like things couldn't get worse, she began to have intense contractions weeks before the baby's due date. With the pregnancy now at risk, she was put on bed rest for those final weeks just as I was starting to walk and eat like a human again. To make matters even worse: It was a record-setting hot July and the AC went out. I couldn't believe it. Two surgeries, one high-risk pregnancy, and no money to fix the AC. How were we ever going to bounce back from this?

Nevertheless, we made it through. About two months later, our precious son Luke was born. We were both elated. We now had more motivation than ever to work our way out of the situation we were in. But the first few months with a newborn baby are never easy, and unfortunately Luke had colic, which meant that at our house, no one slept. Ever.

We later discovered Luke was on the autistic spectrum. He was high-functioning, but it caused him to sleep horribly and have digestive challenges that kept him up all night. With all the financial, health, and family challenges, our marriage was tested like never before too. It felt like everything I had worked for and dreamed of had been smashed into a million little pieces. In almost every way, I felt hopeless.

In short, life hit me like a ton of bricks!

So why am I sharing this nightmare story with you? Because for better or worse, I've learned that these are the experiences that make up who you are. My sincere goal is that these glimpses into my life will help you learn from my journey and stay the course on your own path, no matter what life throws at you.

I didn't realize how good I had it until my cash and career all disappeared. But having everything crumble down around me taught me a few things that have helped me navigate my business to the level of success it has reached today. Last year my team at Better Homes and Gardens Real Estate sold more than 850 homes. And we did it without sacrificing our souls, our mental health, or our family life. But of course, it didn't happen overnight.

The first significant mindset shift I learned during this time of struggle was the way I defined "opportunity." Some people have more opportunities than others, but *all* of us can take advantage of the opportunities we are presented with. In baseball, we can't control the pitch being thrown at us, but we can control how focused we are when we swing the bat, how hard we swing the bat, and how well we turn our body into the swing. Candidly, I had so many opportunities given to me early in life that I didn't realize how fortunate I was. It took me losing so much in business and life to see how good I had had it over the years. This "don't know what you got till it's gone" lesson in opportunity-taking proved to be a pivotal mindset shift. It's had—and continues to have—an impact on literally every area of my life.

For the first time in my life, I became incredibly grateful each time I was given a chance in business and sales. The suffering had changed my view of an opportunity. No matter how large or small, any new opportunity that came across my desk was exciting. This experience has helped me train my sales team and their mindset for success and a lack of complaining.

When a salesperson falls into the trap of complaining about their leads or the demands of the job, they tend to lose their edge. But when you're grateful, positive, and optimistic, you tend to outsell your coworkers without even trying. I've watched real estate agents gather together and complain about their leads, the team, commission splits, and anything else under the sun. This type of thinking will lower your sales performance every time.

Have you ever noticed that when you are shopping for a specific type of car, whatever the car is, you see it everywhere? For example, if I said I wanted a Chevy Tahoe and began researching them, I would see those Chevy Tahoes everywhere I went. Similarly, once you connect with other salespeople who are negative, you are changing your perspective on how you see the world of sales around you. If a prospect says they are not interested in buying a home, you mistakenly remind yourself of what your negative friends just discussed concerning the "poor market" or "bad leads," so you believe this is a bad prospect and continue to spiral into an ongoing negative mindset. If your friends were positive and encouraged you to have more positivity, you would find yourself dealing with the person who says "I am not interested" in a completely different way. You would be genuinely hopeful you might help them find what they were looking for and genuinely confident that they would choose to work with you because you're an amazing agent.

This might not be something you've considered before. In many cases, negative thinking tends to creep into our subconscious without us even realizing it. But looking back on my life, I can now identify countless times my negative outlook prevented me from taking advantage of a great opportunity. If I would have been as grateful for every opportunity then as I am now, I would have looked at the crash of 2008 completely different. I was trying to work my business the way it had always been, but the industry was changing. I was used to putting a sign in the yard and people basically begging me to sell them a home. Instead of bemoaning the fact that those days were over, I should have begun looking at additional opportunities. I could have begun working to get REO accounts or manage rental properties. I could have researched grant opportunities and passed out flyers regarding new government opportunities. I didn't do any of these things. Instead, I let my real estate career die on the vine and incurred massive amounts of debt as a result.

Actionable Takeaways in This Chapter:

Be positive when your friends are negative. They will either become positive with you or they won't want to talk to you as much, because they want someone to be as negative as they are. Either way, your sightline will be clear of toxicity and focused on the next opportunity.

Be grateful. I wasn't grateful for the new opportunities the industry was about to catapult me into, and as a result, I incurred tremendous amounts of debt and stress waiting for things to go back to the way they were. Being ungrateful also caused me to act from a place of entitlement, where I was completely resistant to (and therefore completely unprepared for) change.

When an opportunity is given to you, give it everything you have. Taking it back to the baseball analogy, "You don't know how many solid pitches you'll get in life, so when you see one, swing for the fences!" One of my favorite quotes from Richard Branson, the founder of Virgin Group, which owns four hundred companies is: "If somebody offers you an amazing opportunity but you are not sure you can do it, say yes—then learn how to do it later." Opportunity in business is everything!

2.

LEARNING TO LISTEN

DURING THE ECONOMIC downturn, I was forced to look for additional work to support my family. On a cold February day in 2009, I got ready for my first job fair. I remember going to a store to buy a faux leather folio and fancy parchment paper for my résumé, hoping this would seal the deal on my future. I had a friend who worked for a very large shipping and logistics company that would have a booth at the event, and I was hoping to capitalize on that friendship to obtain a job there. Honestly, I was scrambling for anything at this point. The logistics company booth was going to be my first stop.

I walked into the building and was immediately blown away by the sheer number of people in attendance.

I had to literally push my way through a sea of people to get in front of the hiring manager. As I nudged the last person in my way, asking them to move to the side, I anxiously approached the hiring desk. I was finally able to hand the hiring manager my résumé, but there was such a loud roar of commotion that I barely received a thank-you from her. The manager quickly glanced at my résumé and then was distracted by another potential candidate asking a question.

This interchange was very discouraging. After all, this booth was first on my list. I had gotten up early, bought the best résumé paper I could find, and pushed my way to the front of the line. But apparently having several degrees in theology and business didn't translate into the logistics industry very well. Still, I was hoping my friendship with someone there would help me get my foot in the door. Feeling rejected and directionless, I continued to walk past the various booths hoping to find someone who would speak with me.

About fifteen minutes and three to four awkward hellos later, I came to a booth for a company that sold steel buildings. At first I didn't think there was much of a reason to speak with them about their job offering because I had no experience in steel, construction, or anything remotely close to this industry. Luckily, the hiring manager was incredibly outgoing. He loudly said hello and waved me over. The company was looking for inside salespeople who were outbound phone reps who would be required to sell their $15,000 to $45,000 steel buildings. I knew how to talk to people, so I was immediately interested in the position. Thirty days later I had my second interview with the CMO. He was super engaging, motivating, polished, and smart. It's funny to reflect on this now, but I was so impressed by his BMW 3 series and professional demeanor that I wanted to be part of this team. He told me about the massive number of people who had applied for the role and said he would get back to me if there was an opportunity. A few days later, I was offered a full-time position, which I eagerly accepted.

The first week on the job was training about the buildings—the technology we were using and the scripts that would work best to sell them. My first official day on the phone was an incredibly cold one, and I was sitting right by the front door. It was one of those cold winter days that literally makes your bones shiver. Shivering for eight hours wasn't exactly fun, but I was focused on doing whatever I had to do to support my family.

My time at the steel building company was definitely rewarding, albeit very challenging. Not only did I have the ego blow of wearing a headset for the first time to make calls, plus a small cubicle near the front door with no privacy, now I also had to try to convince people to talk about an inquiry they had made online a year or two previously. Company policy for a new employee was to work the old leads others had never attempted to capitalize on. I remember sitting in the boardroom with all of the new recruits. It was crowded, the dry-erase board was stained from years of dry-erase motivational quotes, and it was early enough that you could smell the alcohol on some of the sales guys from the night before. To say I was out of my element was an understatement.

The sales manager was stereotypical and knew how to speak to the salespeople with powerful, loud descriptions on how to be successful in this role. He attempted to motivate us by describing what it felt like to make $100,000 a year. He passionately described the types of cars we would drive, the types of homes we could buy, and even what kind of wife we could all entice with his approach to sales. (Yes, you read that right.) If we sold buildings the way our manager was recommending, we could have just about everything we could ever imagine.

I don't really think anyone left the room that day feeling particularly motivated; however, one of the items that our manager touched on that day is something that has always stuck with me. He said: "When selling buildings, we need to help the person find out what they want to buy and how one of our products will meet their needs perfectly." The way we were told to do this was to carefully listen to what the person said as well as what they didn't say in order to help us connect with the person on a deep and meaningful level, so as to gain trust. Once the prospect trusted us, my manager explained loudly, we could then meet their building needs. He then emphatically pronounced, "All you have to do is *listen*!"

Those first few weeks, the product was so brand-new in my mind that I didn't feel confident going deep on any of the science behind how the buildings were made while on the phone. So when I heard about the strong focus on listening, I was extremely relieved. I don't really have an engineer's mind and felt that I was at a disadvantage for this reason. When you say you want a twenty-by-twenty garage, that doesn't really mean anything to me. So when I was told I needed to really listen, I started to get it. I could just let the customer talk to me and react accordingly. Sounds easy, right?

I promptly went back to my ice-cold desk near the front door, put on my worn and scratchy headset, and got to work. My first challenge was that people didn't seem to answer the phone. Most of my calls went to voicemail. When someone finally did answer, I was so nervous that I overanxiously did the greeting. I'd use a super-excited and higher-pitched voice, as if the person had just won a prize. With this overly animated voice, I attempted to speak with them about a building they had inquired about two to three years ago. As you can imagine, this approach did not generate results.

Prospects would hang up on me within the first one to two seconds. I didn't even have a chance to listen, let alone pitch. Each time a person would hang up, tell me they were not interested, or yell at me and say, "You people won't stop calling. *Stop!*" I could feel the sweat on my forehead, my heart would race, and my confidence would slip away. After several days of this, I was starting to feel the pressure to perform. The sales team didn't give you new leads until you started selling. I knew if I didn't sell a building soon, I wouldn't be able to keep this job for long. Ironically, it was around that time I seriously wanted to quit. I was superuncomfortable and simply not accustomed to having to work so hard to get someone to like me. I was extremely discouraged.

But what choice did I have? Due to the market crash and my desire to meet our basic needs, such as groceries and the mortgage, I went back to work the next day with a newfound determination (or you could call it desperation). I decided that for the next person who actually answered the phone, I would stop trying so hard and just start the call with something along the lines of, "This is Barry with XYZ Building company. Did you ever find an XYZ building?"

To my surprise, the first person I tried this with actually answered my question. Because it worked the first time, I kept doing it over and over again. To be clear, I didn't sell a building that day. But I did start to have substantive conversations regularly, which was a huge boost to my confidence. I knew it was only a matter of time before I made a sale. Unfortunately for me, my sales manager wasn't impressed that I was motivated. He was only impressed with sales. By the sixth selling day at the company, I still hadn't sold anything. Now, it was really starting to bother me.

By day seven, my luck had finally changed. If my memory serves me correctly, I was the second newly hired salesperson to sell a building within my batch of hires. I pretty much gave it away. My commission was around twenty dollars, but I didn't care. I was just so excited I sold something. I learned a valuable lesson during those first few weeks: people love to be heard and feel validated.

So many times, salespeople go right into "objection handling" as we like to phrase it. Often we do not listen; we just try to prove them wrong quickly, hoping to sell the product. But people want to work with someone who understands them. If they aren't feeling heard, they won't trust you. Not only that; you aren't going to be able to motivate someone unless you know what their real motivation is. The only way to uncover that motivation is by listening intently.

These days when I'm coaching my team, I always recommend a few methods to make the person feel heard over the phone. The first involves validating the person's concern, desire, or experience right off the bat. I typically recommend that we agree with the person as best as we can by repeating back what they said, repeating their name in your response to them, making your connection personal in nature, and giving some kind of affirming response to help them feel understood.

Sample Conversation:

Me: "Hi, John! This is Barry Jenkins with Better Homes and Gardens. I noticed a few homes caught your eye online and I wanted to see if anything about those homes stood out, good or bad."

Prospect: "Hello. I am just browsing. I don't want to buy until aliens land in my backyard and give me down payment assistance!"

Me: "I would want to wait for a down payment from aliens too, if I knew they were coming soon with cash! That makes total sense, John. (Note: Doesn't addressing their name here create a personal connection?) So when you do receive the down payment help, what would you like to change about your current home? Maybe a bigger yard for aliens to land in!"

I'm obviously using a ridiculous example of how to affirm a person who gave a crazy reason not to buy yet. But if you pay close attention to my response, I affirm them and identify/agree with their concerns and repeat their name to warm my statement to them. From there, move on to the next part of the conversation, which dives deeper into the process. I recommend using a phrase to keep the conversation going after the person responds to you by saying something like, "That's super interesting! Tell me more about how you came to that conclusion!" This normally opens the person up to continue sharing details about their home search. Questions like these were *everything* for me at the steel building company, and they translated perfectly to real estate sales too.

Verbiage such as "How did you come to that conclusion?" makes it easy for a person to elaborate their desires and stay on the subject of home buying or selling. It would be a complete waste of time for me to spend twenty minutes listening to this person tell me about different kinds of aliens. Be careful how far you go attempting to connect with a prospect. Some salespeople misuse gaining trust by trying to become instant BFFs while on the phone. I'm not advocating for rushing the person off the phone, however; I'm on the phone with this person to help them navigate what will probably be the largest financial transaction of their life. They need me to be focused and give good counsel. This is what I like to call "active listening." Passive listening is letting the person talk with no engagement or direction from me. Active listening is taking what the person says, making them feel heard, and then applying what they're saying to the greater goal of buying a home. This is overwhelmingly a core desire of most consumers: They want someone to help them navigate the big picture and give direction as needed.

I've had the privilege of working as an executive at Ylopo for four years now, all while running a top-performing real estate team. I've had many projects that I enjoyed working on that were different, challenging and, most of all, rewarding. One such project entailed rewriting all of the scripts our AI texting platform was using to qualify leads. We call her Raiya. It was a gargantuan task that spanned four months, eight hundred to nine hundred different texts, and a reworking of an entire conversational flow for multiple types of leads. After the first thirty days of implementation with my new scripts, we were able to review the outcome. We reviewed ninety thousand text messages sent in thirty days, and my revisions doubled Raiya's conversation to appointment rate, need agent callback rate, and decreased the "not interested" rating by 50 percent. I utilized the subject of this book in my rationale for messaging.

As I alluded to previously, sometimes we attempt to be the person's best friend while on the phone, and this is misguided at best. I don't know about you, but I don't have enough time for my real friends. The thought that a random salesperson is going to connect with me on a deep and meaningful level after a five-minute chat is pretty ridiculous. I have had several agents on my teams over the years who would regularly trumpet the fact they had had *so* many great conversations the day before. They would beam with pride as they told the rest of the team a prospect's favorite color, favorite movie, what they wanted to do when they retired, even how many brothers and sisters they had! After they presented the laundry list of facts they'd collected, they would typically try to drive home the point that they had a great call by sharing and connecting with the prospect. They might say something like, "We even buy groceries at the same store and we both love the movie *Rocky*!" To which I typically reply, "That's all great! But what kind of home do they want?"

My agents who are excited about connecting on a personal level oftentimes do not have much information on the prospect's home search needs. They may have some information but nowhere near those agents who are focused on eagerly helping the buyer find a home. I remember one agent going into a crazy amount of detail about their phone conversations from every meeting. She would list detailed stories and facts about her leads. "John loves eating Italian for dinner with his wife after their son Johnny plays baseball." At first, I was excited to see my agent connecting with so many people. But as the months went by, she wasn't selling more than one deal every three to four months. Once I realized she wasn't performing, I decided to dig into her process for the phone call. After several discussions, I realized she wasn't listening with the goal of helping them with their home-buying needs; she was listening to connect.

Because of this, she consistently was connecting with people on the wrong level, and the result was the prospect would have one long conversation with her but wouldn't respond to her follow-up calls, emails, or texts.

Listening for "the sake of listening" isn't contributing to your end goal or your prospect's end goal. Listening to "analyze and give good feedback" is what the prospect needs from you.

Actionable Takeaways in This Chapter:

Listening and opportunity are two sides of the same coin. By asking a question and just listening, you open up your opportunity to connect with and guide a prospect in their home-buying journey.

Make the person feel heard. Use active listening and affirming statements.

Don't connect just to connect. Connect for the purpose of helping the prospect get their real estate needs met.

3.

CREATING AN OPPORTUNITY FOR YOU TO BE INVOLVED

ARMED WITH A new appreciation for opportunity and an effective listening-centric sales approach, I finally became the top salesperson at the steel building company and was on track to make a solid annual salary. However, the grind of fifty- to sixty-hour workweeks plus the task of calling all day, every day, was starting to get to me. I was eating junk food for three "meals" a day just to comfort myself. The salespeople around me regularly had inappropriate images on their computers, vulgar music and jokes being shared, and they would all lie through their teeth to make a sale. Sure, they were nice to me, but I didn't feel proud of myself at the end of each day. It was one of those jobs that made you want to take a moral shower when you got home, and there were numerous gray areas I would have to navigate daily.

One such gray area was in regards to creating urgency. This was normally a huge topic at sales meetings. Management would call a "creating urgency" meeting to discuss how to create urgency for the big month-end sales push. The most glaring method of creating urgency was when we would receive an inbound call. We called those "overhead leads." (I'm not sure why we called them that, but they were the best leads the business offered.)

When an overhead lead came in, the team would have one of the top salespeople take an inbound call and answer the potential customer's technical questions. From there, we would somehow have to segue into a buying conversation. The prospects would typically thank us for the information, then attempt to rush off the phone. But at this company, if you weren't able to keep the conversation going with an overhead lead, management wouldn't give you many more opportunities. Most people don't buy a $10,000 or $20,000 garage after a twenty-minute phone call, so warming them up was key. We were told that if we didn't create the need to buy during the "create urgency" call, we weren't doing our job the way the company required. To add more pressure to the scenario, if we didn't close the person right then and there, the likelihood of keeping them as a customer was slim to none. Needless to say, pulses would quicken every time an inbound call came in.

The main way the steel building company taught us to close inbound calls was to create and share an urgent offer with the customer that would have to be taken advantage of right away (re: sale/discount). We were instructed to advise the customer that there might be a good deal in the warehouse and if they would hold for a few minutes, we would check for them. We would make them wait three to four minutes while we listened on hold. When we came back to the phone, we would tell the prospect some ridiculous story about an order for a thirty-by-fifty-size building (for example, a big garage or workshop) being canceled and we had to chop it up and sell it for parts. As the story went, it "*just* so happened" that the remainder of the building was the exact size this person needed. As the sales method would go, we emphasized that the prospect on the other end of the phone could get an amazing deal because of these leftover parts.

First, let me note, this *always* worked if the person was a serious buyer. Second, we were identifying with the consumer's desire to find a good deal. We would offer the normal price, then offer the sales price, then ask if the buyer wanted us to check if our manager could lower it even more. We then would close with, "If I can get you somewhere in your budget, are you in a position to put down a deposit now and pay the garage off when it's delivered in several months?" If they said yes, that was a sale. Every. Single. Time.

This really messed with my conscience. Because there weren't really any extra buildings, nor a warehouse with leftover parts. We were making up stories to create a need to buy immediately. Ultimately, I had to decide if I was going to stay at the steel building place or go somewhere that wouldn't make me question my own ethics every day. After about a year, I finally left to go into the insurance industry. Somehow I thought that because insurance was a licensed professional industry, it would be easier to sell the product. I mean, everyone needs insurance, right? Wrong. Have you ever tried to convince someone they are going to die someday and need to prepare beforehand? I have, and it sucks. At the insurance company, we didn't receive inbound leads as we did at the steel building company. We had to make outbound calls to current policyholders and offer to do an insurance review. During the insurance review, we would try to strategically bring up the life insurance topic with something like, "Hi, Mr. Smith, we're calling because we haven't reviewed your insurance and we want to make sure you are getting all of your discounts. Is there a time in the next week we can meet?" This method worked, because everyone wants more discounts. The challenge with this approach was you had to change the focus from saving money to spending money while in front of the family.

Once in front of the client, we would use a brochure that was essentially a life insurance calculation tool. It added up the costs of different things, such as your mortgage balance, college education for the kids, living expenses, and other things that would come up if the breadwinner in the family suddenly passed away. It then would multiply most of those amounts by the number of dependents you had and the number of years until those dependents were adults. This was a tough conversation to have!

One day I had a weeknight meeting with a younger family. The wife had scheduled the appointment and the husband had no idea we were meeting. You could tell he wasn't thrilled I was there. Not that he was overly rude—at least not at first. You could just tell he was exhausted. It was around 7:00 p.m. that evening when I entered the home, and he was still wearing his work uniform. By the logo on his shirt, it was clear he worked at a place that does copy and printing work. The family had just finished dinner when I walked in.

I went over a few of the discounts they could obtain and then transitioned to life insurance. As I started to shift to the reason I was really there, the husband shut me down abruptly. He said they already had coverage through his workplace, so there was no need to discuss buying any additional policies. He then said something that really struck a nerve: "I thought you were here to help us save money. Why are you trying to sell us another policy?" I tried to pivot the conversation by stating the obvious, "Well, sir, you are going to die one day and I wanted to inform you . . ."

He wasn't having it. He said he'd like to move on and didn't want to discuss it anymore. The guy was obviously tired and not prepared for this subject. However, he had cut to the real issue at hand: I was pretending to offer one service, but the real reason I was in their home that evening was to make a sale by creating a need for more life insurance. It was a bait and switch. Here I was in yet another sales position that made me feel like I was tricking people into buying something.

Similar to the steel building company, the insurance industry taught me to create a need by offering discounts and exposing a "need" for more. In both industries, the customer was not prepared to make a decision or buy the product being sold. Because of the story and pitch I was taught, I was able to open up a dialogue about why the person I was speaking to should buy the product. The challenge I had with life insurance was that I like to make people happy. Attempting to get someone to pay money in case they died did not make people happy. They were normally uncomfortable and frustrated. I lasted about a year in that sales position before I went back into real estate full-time.

After a month or two back in the swing of real estate, I realized how much easier it was to sell a home. Everyone wants a roof over their head. Zillow had really settled nicely into our market by that time, and I was able to capture many people (you might call them leads) shopping for a home online. After a few months of calling people who were requesting information on Zillow, I realized that I had an incredible opportunity: I didn't have to create a need for them to buy a home, nor did I have to create urgency for them to buy a home as soon as possible. Both of the specific concerns I had at the last two sales jobs were totally removed when I went back into real estate. Fast-forward two years later to 2012, and I was selling 125+ homes a year with no support staff. It was bananas!

As time went on, Zillow and Realtor.com leads became too expensive to build a team on, and I was forced to find alternate lead sources. I began to try my hand on leads generated from Google and Facebook. These leads were *much* cheaper than the online search portals, but the challenge with these leads was that many of them didn't know what they wanted in a home. Contrary to a Zillow-sourced lead, these consumers were beginning their research and many times didn't know in what price, style, location, or timeframe they were buying a home. Like many agents today, I was at a loss for how to develop these opportunities into actionable business. Over the next several years, I found myself really crystalizing my approach with these types of leads. What I learned in these few years comprised the beginning framework for much of this book, and my record-breaking years to follow.

Let's take an example: John begins searching for homes on Google in his hometown of Big City Ville. He's toying with the idea of no longer renting an apartment and buying something reasonable. It's been four years since he graduated college, and he was just promoted to assistant manager at his bank. He feels like buying a home would be the logical next step in his adulthood. When he starts searching on Google, an ad showing waterfront homes in Big City Ville pops up and he clicks the link. He's always dreamed of owning a boat, so the waterfront aspect of the properties are very appealing. When he lands on the page of waterfront homes, he sees an option to adjust the price. He's not sure what he can qualify for, but he knows he can't afford the million-dollar property the website is displaying. He starts to input his price adjustments and a box pops up asking him to register. John really doesn't want to register, but he sees a few homes in the background that catch his eye, so he goes ahead and starts to fill out the information. His Google Chrome browser prefills his work contact info into the form on the website, so he just hits "enter" so he can get back to looking at the properties. Shortly after submitting his info, and while he's still browsing the photos he likes, John begins to hear his cell phone buzz. He sees a text message and then an email from the agent who owns the website he's on.

Pop quiz! Given the preceding scenario, what type of script or messaging do you think makes the most sense?

Option #1. "Hi, John! This is Mike with ABC Realty. I saw you registered to view waterfront homes and I wanted to speak to you concerning this. I just listed a home on Pond View Lake and think you would love it! Can I call now?"

Option #2. "Hi, John! This is Mike with ABC Realty. I saw you registered to view waterfront homes. I'm sure you aren't looking to buy right away, but I'd like to chat regarding your goals of buying one day, whenever that might be. Also, there are two things I think you should start to think about to prepare yourself. Do you have five minutes to discuss this over the next day or so?"

It's so clear when you read it like this, right? Yet most agents lead with trying to shove a house down the person's throat. Also, Option #2 will help you gain more traction in this scenario than Option #1 because it's attempting to add value by teaching the prospect something he doesn't know.

By providing information that teaches the person about the process in a way that shows the prospect they don't know as much as the agent, you create an inherent need for your service.

Unfortunately, agents are typically only comfortable discussing specific properties, as in Option #1. When the prospect doesn't know what they want yet, agents don't really know how to add any value. I am convinced that agents who are able to convert top-of-funnel leads who are early on in their real estate journey will be the ones who make a great living over the next decade. The days of only working with people who want to move quickly just isn't viable. To continue selling many homes, you will need to learn the skill of talking with people who are just beginning the process.

Actionable Takeaways in This Chapter:

Don't waste your time on sleazy urgency tactics. Creating urgency can be done in a way that doesn't scare the prospect.

Don't rush your prospects. Using a script that doesn't focus on the person buying a home right away tends to be more effective because you gain more trust (and deals) over time.

Add value first. Creating a need for you is the key to speaking with someone early in their buying or selling process.

PART TWO

4.

CREATING A GENUINE NEED

GOD BLESS MY wife for allowing me to take the massive risk of going back into real estate. If you recall, we had more than $50,000 of consumer credit debt from the real estate market crash of 2008. Every penny counted, and if this didn't work out for us, it would absolutely destroy us financially. My wife's support was a huge part of why I was able to take the final step back into real estate full-time. My dad, who owned our brokerage, was also instrumental in supporting me through this transition as well. He would sometimes show homes for me, help with listings, and simply be my hands and feet while I worked towards transitioning back into the industry.

Due to my financial circumstance, and the fact that I did not want to go back to telling people they were going to die for a living, I felt a massive sense of urgency in closing every deal and converting every lead, listing, and conversation into business. I was tempted daily to become a high-pressure salesperson. With the last couple of years being a more cutthroat sales environment, it was almost part of my DNA now.

Thankfully, my faith and ethics checked me into not tricking or lying to people to get them to buy a home. The thing about choosing to do what's right or wrong is that it's not a singular decision. It's a moment-by-moment, day-by-day, month-by-month, and year-by-year decision. I consistently struggled with choosing to put others' interests above my own when it came to selling people homes during this transition back into full-time real estate.

Like most struggles, this day-to-day challenge produced amazing results and molded me into a new kind of salesperson. One who was still fast, focused, and efficient yet would never lie or guilt people into buying a product they didn't want. I was teaching, not pushing or pressuring, people into buying.

The next four points are approaches that enabled me to keep my conscience clear while exceeding all the sales goals I ever dreamed of. Over the course of just one year, I went from selling ten homes a month consistently to twenty, and have remained there for the rest of my career. From that point on, I never looked back financially. All my debts were paid off, we had an abundance of income, and finally the other areas of my life started to fall into place.

I recommend reading the rest of this chapter a few times. Digest it and incorporate it into your dialogue on the phone, in conversations, and in scripting via text or email, and all automation platform content you use should have these principles interwoven with it. If you use the following information and rationale when prospecting, you will absolutely crush it. I am certain of it!

Point One: Your Prospects Don't Know What They Don't Know

Most buyers and sellers you speak with are totally ignorant of the process of buying or selling a home. They do actually need you; they just don't know it. Don't trust their opinion of your worth, because you're the expert, not them!

When I speak to an agent who isn't selling many homes, they are typically exasperated, frustrated, and ready to stop spending money on marketing and/or buying leads. I have spent countless hours training individual agents, small teams, and even some of the largest teams in the country through my role as the Ylopo realtor in residence. In this role, I noticed a trend that if a Ylopo user happens not to be doing well on the platform, the user will say something such as, "The leads are bad. The info is bad. No one is picking up the phone; I think I just need to cancel." To which I thoughtfully ask, "What success have you had with online marketing in your business over the last few years? Has there been a lead source you have done well with?" More often than not, agents tell me they haven't really had much success with any online lead-generating platform, but occasionally they'll say Zillow or Realtor.com has been helpful. The norm for most agents I speak to is they are not successful with online leads and they have had the bulk of their transactions come from their sphere and past client referrals. Week after week I speak with agents who go from one online lead-generation platform to another. Platform A promises two new features to help you crush it. They don't do well on Platform A, so they switch to Platform B. Platform B promises to do all the work, and all you have to do is show homes. When that doesn't work out, they are then forwarded on to Platform C. Most struggling agents run their business this way. All of them are searching for a system that will help them grow their business beyond just working their sphere of influence.

The challenge with an agent who is used to working only with contacts who either know them or have been referred by someone who knows them, is the fact that the person asking for help has a true real estate need. By the time someone asks for an agent, whether directly to the agent or indirectly through a friend, they typically have some kind of real estate need. I can't overstate how significant this is for agents when working with leads generated on the Internet for home buyers and sellers. If you're only talking to people who know what they want to a certain degree, you won't be comfortable speaking to someone who doesn't know what they need. Rather than helping someone navigate their needs, agents continue to be perplexed as to what to say to someone who is unsure of their needs.

An example of the "not knowing what they want" type of buyer would be a home buyer who wants to one day buy a home and is simply browsing on your website. This buyer doesn't have a plan and quite frankly isn't much interested in creating one. If you call a buyer who is in this position, you will most likely receive the response, "I'm just looking" or "I'm not serious." When an agent hears this, they write the person off almost immediately. Most agents will end the call with something lame like, "Can I call you next month?" or "Can I email you some information?" We mainly respond in this way because the person doesn't seem like they want to talk to us. We can feel it on the other end of the phone. It's the overwhelming feeling of rejection as the lead is attempting to end the call as quickly as possible. Due to this feeling of rejection, many agents end up mirroring the lead by trying to get off the phone quickly. They can feel the resistance, and it makes them uncomfortable. The message we send to that buyer is the agent isn't relevant until the need is identified by the buyer. We also send the message that we will just keep contacting them and hope that we might happen to catch them when they are finally ready.

When comparing the person who doesn't know what they want and doesn't think they need an agent right now to a buyer who has been asking their friends and family for the name of an agent because they'd like to start looking at homes and learn more about the home-buying process, it's no surprise that agents are only looking to have one type of conversation. A buyer who is starting to get an idea of what they want in a home will appreciate being asked if they have been approved for a mortgage. Someone just starting the process will not appreciate that question as much. Further, a person just starting out will typically answer the question "What kind of home do you want?" with a quick "I don't know. I am just looking right now." When a lead has this type of response, agents take that as a rejection rather than realizing that the person has no idea how to answer the agent's questions. If recognized by the agent early in the conversation, hearing the lead not discuss their needs in any substantive and concise way is a glaring signal that this is someone who needs more hand-holding. They did, in fact, register on your website, so there must be some degree of interest.

Going back to my conversations with agents during my role as Ylopo realtor in residence, I typically would ask a rhetorical question to help the agent learn a new approach by thinking about the conversation from the buyer's perspective. I would typically ask the agent something such as, "Are you only valuable to a prospective buyer when they know what kind of home they want? Further, are you only valuable at opening the door to the home and writing the contract?" I've never had an agent answer that question with, "True, I'm not valuable in any other area."

In our heads we think we are guides and counselors, but in practice we are really restaurant servers. For most agents, they are only effective if the client knows what they want and asks for help, and we meet the need. Much like the server who brings a large Coke when requested by the patron in the restaurant, most realtors are only good at responding to clearly defined needs by the consumer. The core difference between a guide and a server at a restaurant is that a guide takes an active role in preparation and planning. I grabbed a quick definition of guidance from Google, and here's what I found: "Advice or information aimed at resolving a problem or difficulty, especially as given by someone in authority." If we truly are the guide in real estate, we must realize that we are the authority on the subject. This consideration of authority leads me to point number two.

Point Two: Be a Resource!

You show value to a prospect by actually sharing knowledge. I have discovered over the years that by teaching the person things they don't know about home buying, you are displaying to the prospect that you are valuable.

If this entire book was only made up of me telling you about the many different ways I was good at real estate, you likely wouldn't get much from it. However, you will (hopefully) value this book because I am teaching you things to help you expand your business. So you value this book not because I simply say that you should value what I teach but because it contains valuable information that makes you want to keep reading!

I want you to have the same approach with every lead you speak with. Provide so much direction, information, and insight into what the person should be doing in order to accomplish their goals that a person would be crazy to choose anyone else. I've built my career on this idea. Even after a ten- to fifteen-minute monologue with a prospect in which I shared valuable information, I would typically say, "I know I just shared lots of information with you akin to word vomit, and I apologize. I really love helping people make this process easy, and once I get started, I can't stop! Do you have any questions about what I just went over?" This statement was my attempt to use humor to reinforce the fact that I just taught them a great deal of information and wanted to be sensitive to the fact that they might need some further explanation.

I'd like to reference my last point for a moment to help give context to this current thought. If you ask a person if they are approved for a mortgage and they quickly want to get off the phone and say they are just looking, what would your response be? If you use the typical response of, "Can I email you listings and call next month to see how it's coming along?" you won't get to the place of teaching the person anything. There is nothing in your conversation that would make someone want to receive an email from you because they haven't yet understood that you're a valuable source of information.

Think about this for a moment: What you're really asking when you ask a prospect if they are preapproved is what they know about the mortgage process. When they don't know enough and rush you off the phone, you then tell them you will email them later. Isn't that ridiculous? You're raising an important topic that person genuinely needs to learn about, and because they don't realize how important it is, you respond as if it is not important by getting off the phone quickly. You're basically teaching the person by your actions that what you said isn't important, because if it were, you would have conducted yourself much differently.

Point Three: People Don't Have a Plan! (Even When They Say They Do!)

The prospect needs you today, not in twelve months. It's not unusual to hear a prospect say they want to buy "next year." In U.S. culture, if it's affordable and I want it, I buy it. I'm not saying this is necessarily a good thing, but it is very much how our society operates. Most prospects you speak with will say they are planning to buy a home in about a year. I recently saw a survey that stated 70 percent of people fail at their New Year's resolution by January 11 and 92 percent by February 1. As a culture, we don't plan things a year ahead and actually maintain our focus on said goal. Again, I'm not saying this is a good or a bad thing; it's simply the reality of the world in which we live. When someone tells you that they want to buy a home in twelve months, you need to realize there is at least a 92 percent chance they aren't going to stick to their plan or goal.

In most cases, they don't really have a goal or plan at all. More often than not, the prospect doesn't know what kind of home they want and are early on in the process. I have further discovered over my twenty-one-year career that when a prospect doesn't have an overt and immediate real estate need (e.g., "Can we see 123 Smith Street tonight?"), the prospect doesn't truly feel they need to be speaking with you yet. In this scenario, your attempts to build rapport on a personal level will not work.

Remember, you aren't selling a house when you talk to someone who is early on in their buying journey; you are selling your value. By being valuable to the prospect, we will speed up the long-term nurture, going from nine to twelve months down to three to four months. Our group of teams sold more than nine hundred homes in 2019 using this simple idea. If done right, you're helping dispel confusion while shortening the learning curve of buying/selling a home so that your prospect can get on with their life. I will go over how you can quickly teach and add value in detail in the next chapter. For now, it's important that you recognize your prospects need you today and they don't actually have a plan for tomorrow.

Point Four: Find Your 5 Percent

As an industry, we tend to have a guru culture mindset. We think things such as, "If I can learn from XYZ coach, I can really become a mega agent just like them." Without realizing, of course, that XYZ coach attempts to make their techniques hyperadvanced in order to make your purchase of their training program more valuable. Don't get me wrong. I'm not trying to take away from an honest teacher and their value. (After all, you're reading my book right now.) However, if you simply will go to work daily and follow a set plan that you know will produce results, you are bound to become successful.

I train my teams to focus on the five out of one hundred attempts that will end up being potential clients.

I'm not saying five out of a hundred will go look at homes this month. I'm saying five out of one hundred contacts will probably transact in real estate in the next six to twelve months. If you can connect with five out of a hundred people this month, you have an amazing and vibrant career in real estate ahead of you.

This also means that there will be ninety-five times someone won't answer, won't be interested, or won't think they need you right now. When I'm coaching other agents, I often find that they will call around ten to fifteen people a month then get disappointed because none of those fifteen people are interested in speaking. Most agents aren't even connecting with 5 percent of their database per month. This is really where the rubber meets the road: If you don't talk to more people in a week, you simply won't convert many online leads. The key is having more opportunities every month. Really, if I just got this one point across to you, I think you'd almost instantly start making more money.

Our office recently assisted our agents in setting goals for the next calendar year. We asked each agent how much they wanted to make the following year, then reverse engineered that income goal with the number of times they need to attempt to talk to someone, the number of conversations they need to have, the number of appointments that will most likely come from those conversations and the number of appointments that will lead to written contracts. What was interesting was that some received that initial number of attempted contacts and immediately asked to reduce their income goal. One agent in particular saw that they needed to attempt one thousand texts and five hundred calls per month to make their income goal numbers. This agent immediately said to me, "I don't want to work that hard. What would I make if I called one hundred people a month and texted five hundred?" We discussed the income differences, and this person decided to settle on a lower income goal. While I don't fault someone for setting their income goals at what they want, I do think that not giving something your all is a mistake.

To be clear: ninety-five out of one hundred times, you won't be successful.

The hang-up for most agents is that they just don't believe that if they speak to one hundred people, they will actually get business from it. This really is the core issue and, when dealt with appropriately, can revolutionize your business. When you're receiving leads from any online source, remember that these prospects have contacted *you*. However great or small, they do have some kind of real estate need. Agents get too caught up in the rejection of the ninety-five attempted contacts and fail to recognize that this is the game.

Did you ever do that thing as a kid where you get to go mining for gold? I remember being on a field trip in elementary school in the mountains. The guide taught us the entire gold-mining process and then took us to actually mine for gold in their makeshift river. I remember grabbing an item that looked like a plate and letting the water flow through the screen. The first person to catch a piece of gold would get a free gift from the gift shop. As a naturally competitive person, I already wanted to win. But when I heard we could get a free toy, man, I was so motivated to capture that gold! I was so focused on the prize, I really didn't think about the water or the amount of water flowing through the screen. I was focused on one thing: finding that *gold*!

You see where I'm going with this, right? In many ways, our outbound phone prospecting needs to be like that field trip. We need to treat the nos we receive like water that flows through the screen and not be distracted by it; we need to be laser-focused on finding the gold. If you have this mindset, you'll find your prospecting time will suddenly come alive. You'll be more frequent in your attempts and become more focused to move swiftly past rejection as you stay the course and continue to go for gold.

Each month, I ask my agents to simply find five out of a hundred people who have some kind of intent to buy or sell in the next year. We consider the "buying next year" folks and the "buying next month" folks to be of equal importance to our business. It's not about finding "hot leads." It's not about making a sale. It's finding those five people who need our help, and we hunt for them like we are hunting for gold.

Actionable Takeaways in This Chapter:

Set specific, attainable goals. Stay focused on opportunity, not rejection.

Own your knowledge. Your role as a realtor is to be a resource to your community. Don't shy away from that just because someone isn't preapproved for a mortgage! Show your value in every call, text, and email.

Find five out of one hundred people you can help. Like mining for gold, stay focused on the outcome.

5.

Know Where the Buyer
Is In Their Journey

Now, this might surprise you, but people don't wake up in the morning and simply say, "I think I'm gonna buy a house today." They don't just happen to see a property on your real estate website or on their social media feeds and say, "I'm going to buy this house later today." They usually plan well in advance, going into every detail before deciding to make what is probably the largest purchase of their life.

For example, someone who is checking their Facebook newsfeed and then happens to register on your website probably isn't ready to answer some significant questions about what they want in a home. However, someone who goes to a real estate–specific site such as Zillow and picks out a price range, area, and style of a home is usually ready to discuss their home search to a certain degree. This type of buyer is typically prepared to answer fundamental questions such as, "When do you want to move?" or "What kind of home do you want to buy?"

We've already discussed some of the differences in working with someone from your sphere versus working with someone who doesn't know you yet, but in this chapter, I want to go even deeper on the importance of a home buyer's journey. Because knowing where your buyer is in their home-buying process, or where your seller is in their home-selling process, impacts everything about your conversation with them and how you can be helpful.

Many agents find one script or approach that works with one type of lead or scenario and don't know how to adjust it to fit new circumstances or conversations. In a lot of cases, the agents aren't sensitive or aware enough when speaking to the prospect to know where the buyer or seller actually is in their home journey. This results in the typical brush-off from the lead, saying something like, "I'm not interested" or "I'm just looking" or "I'm just browsing." Why? Simply because they aren't prepared to answer the question that is asked of them. The wildest thing about the brush-off response is that it usually isn't due to a prospect's lack of desire for a new home. Most of these people very much would like a home; they just aren't sure what to do next.

What my agents have been trained to do, and it works tremendously well, is asking the lead questions they can answer. We try to ask questions that teach as much as gain information. Socrates, one of the great fathers of philosophy, used this method of teaching by asking questions. Jesus, in the Bible, did the same thing. He would typically ask questions to teach his followers. This method is widely understood to engage the listener's brain, gain more information, and help them to formulate a response.

Instead of asking home buyers what kind of home they want, we will typically ask a question such as, "Out of the homes you saw on my website, is there anything that stood out to you, good or bad?" or "Whenever you decide to move, what are you hoping to change about your current home?" The significance of this question is that even if someone isn't ready to talk about real estate, they will be able to answer because it's just asking them about the experience that they had while browsing your website for a home.

I spoke with a team owner in another state not too long ago. They received more than one thousand leads from a particular lead source, but they hadn't closed anything. Needless to say, the team owner was very frustrated. They'd already spent thousands of dollars generating these leads and were even ready to throw in the towel with that particular lead source.

When the team leader came to me with this scenario, I recommended the question-asking approach: "Maybe you need to start asking questions that the leads can answer so you can determine where you can add value during that first call." A month later, I checked back in with the team owner and found out that of the one hundred leads they had received, six appointments were set to meet the client to discuss their home-buying journey.

It was a tremendous improvement after thirty days, and not surprisingly, the team leader was thrilled at the change in response. Here's the reason I regularly see these kinds of results with just a small change in approach: Instead of going for the quick sale, you opened up a conversation. Instead of pressuring them to buy or sell now, you merely engaged them. A meaningful discussion took place. If you can nurture the kind of communication where you're asking them questions that steer them to the path of discovery, you're going to find that people will value the discussion with you so much more.

Sometimes a person isn't ready to talk about where they are because they aren't prepared to have the conversation. As I've stated before, but again for clarity, you can ask them questions they can answer that will hopefully lead them to figure out what they want. This is by far the best way to start the conversation with a new prospect

Once the conversation has started to go deeper in terms of the buyer's goals and wishes, discussing specific desires in a home purchase is very important. When someone already has an idea of what they want, whether it's a price or a style, for example, one of the ways you can add value is by giving insight into where they're looking. For example, if you know that they're looking in a specific zip code and price range, you can mention to them anything you know or have discovered about the area they're seeking.

Bringing insight into the area is an example of a way to add tremendous value at the onset of the conversation. The person will start to appreciate the value of getting insights into the market and your opinion. When that person goes to a real estate–specific website ready to answer particular real estate questions, and has a set price in mind, a set neighborhood, and even wants to see a specific house, then that's the lead everybody is looking for.

Many real estate agents are looking for these types of leads—leads who just want to have the door open and need only their agent's service to gain entry. Most active agents want leads that respond favorably to questions and statements such as, "When do you want to meet?" and "When do you want me to open up the home? I'll show it to you. If you like it, I'll help you write an offer." Everybody wants this kind of lead. But new leads are not typically interested in buying right away, nor are they interested in shopping right away. But because we're not paying specific attention to where the person is in their journey, we end up missing the opportunity to show real value to our prospect. We just ask the bottom-of-funnel questions that hopefully find a desperate home buyer ready to move immediately.

The analogy I use for this situation is the top of a mountain. Just think of the summit as buying or selling a home. The agent is standing at the peak, saying, "Come on; I'll help you get ready to buy. Meet me up here at the top of the mountain." But the prospect is still at the bottom of the mountain, and they have to get to the top on their own. Instead of waiting for them to reach the top of the mountain of "ready to buy now," we go down to the bottom of the mountain and instead indicate to them, "We know you're not ready, we're glad that you're not ready, we're going to celebrate that and partner with you from the beginning of your journey. We'll help you wherever you are today without pushing or stressing you out. We wish to be of whatever value we can be for you today."

By realizing that we shouldn't be discouraged that someone is not yet ready to buy or sell real estate, we protect ourselves against the kind of disappointment that can prevent us from achieving momentum in our real estate careers. Instead we take the opportunity to be relevant to the consumer in their current status. We teach them insights into the market—insights into where they are, regardless of what they think they should be doing.

With this simple shift in mindset, potential home buyers or sellers who have told us they are six to twelve months away from buying or selling a home suddenly want to buy in three to four months! I remember a young military couple who said they were a year away from buying a home because they wanted to save money for a down payment. Rather than discouraging their decision and trying to convince them that they didn't have to do that, we celebrated their being so responsible and how they were saving their money now for their future purchase. We encouraged them in their ventures.

We subtly mentioned to them that there were some ways they could buy and not need as much money. We simply asked, "Are you interested in learning how to save a little bit?"

And since they were in the military, we ended up meeting with them and went over what we call the VIP Military Program. Not only did they not know they can have a zero-down loan using their VA eligibility, but there were other incentives they could receive as well, such as free appraisals and discounts. They ended up wanting to look sooner than they had planned! Within thirty days, they started looking for a home. They ended up closing on a house in ninety days and were so thrilled that they gave us rave reviews.

We did not push them. We did not stress them out. We merely connected with them. In that first conversation, if we had gone for the usual spiels such as, "The interest rates are going up; you need to hurry!" or "There's no better time to buy than now" and tried to use fear to motivate them, we likely would've scared them off completely. They wouldn't have answered our call, and we would've probably blamed the lead source.

And I get it. I like a lead who is ready to have a door opened as much as the next salesperson. But if you can learn how to create more opportunities with people who are early on in the process or funnel, you're going to sell more homes because you'll have more opportunities. But more than that, you're going to help more people, and really, isn't that the main goal? To serve others in your occupation and create scenarios that win for everyone?

I stumbled upon this strategy accidentally by simply helping people. When someone had a legitimate reason in their mind as to why they weren't buying or selling real estate at the moment and I found a way to fix their problem, I would excitedly teach them the solution. I didn't actively study this process and think, "This is a way to get more sales." I loved this process because it felt fun and natural to be of service. It wasn't until years (and several hundreds of transactions later) that I saw it as a method that could also help agents sell more homes.

If you can find a similar motivation to teach and serve others, you can build an incredibly strong sales approach that feels much easier than whatever it is you're doing today to close more deals. And the best part? You can do it with your head held high knowing you're doing right by everyone around you. And in this way, you can be nice and still crush it in sales!

Actionable Takeaways in This Chapter:

Be aware of where the lead is in their journey of buying or selling a home so you can adjust your approach (and your mindset).

Understand that value is relative. What works for your SOI won't work for a brand-new contact. There are no "good" or "bad" leads, just different people with different needs depending on where they are in their real estate journey.

Be motivated to help others. By being motivated to help others and teach them, you can be a very strong salesperson without falling into the trap of being the "stereotypical salesperson."

6.

Know Where The Buyer Is In Their Journey Part Two

In the last chapter, I unpacked the concept of being in touch with where people are in their buying or selling journey. In this chapter, I want to take it a step further by classifying the buying or selling journey into four core categories. These categories will help you in classifying the prospect, engaging the prospect, nurturing the prospect, and eventually selling the prospect a home in a way that feels natural, never forced.

The first category we will review is the early stage buyer who is dreaming of one day buying a home. We'll call this the Dreamer category. People in this category are conceptually starting to consider a purchase or sale of a home but are either too early on or too overwhelmed to actually be ready to buy or sell. Agents typically will call these folks "tire kickers" or "looky-loos." If an agent spends their day talking to these types of buyers, they are typically pretty discouraged. As I noted in the previous chapter, if someone doesn't know what they want yet, they typically think talking to an agent is a complete waste of time. And can you blame them? Dreamers are not interested in seriously looking for a home yet and are even a bit scared to speak with a mortgage person right away. This is likely the largest purchase of their life, and they are trying to make sure they don't mess it up. This causes them to dream about the idea of buying or selling but not really to consider it as something they're able to accomplish at this moment.

Characteristics of a Dreamer:

1) They aren't ready to commit to you (or anyone) because they don't know exactly what they are committing to.

2) They don't think they need to be speaking with you right now. Many Dreamers incorrectly believe that they only need an agent once they've figured out all the details of when, where, and how and only need you to open the door of the home they found on their own.

3) They are scared. They're scared about the amount of money they are spending. They're scared of buying the wrong home. They are scared of making a costly mistake.

Adapting to the characteristics of a Dreamer:

1) Give lots of information. Don't try to get them to commit too quickly, as they aren't yet clear on next steps or the process overall. If you push them, you will scare them away.

2) Start asking some of the questions we've discussed in other chapters to help them figure out where they are in the process: "Have you been

looking for a home long? Do you have a friend in the mortgage business?" Create opportunities to show your value as they come up naturally in the conversation.

3) Don't use fear to motivate the Dreamer. Saying things such as, "If you don't talk to a lender, you might miss out on your dream home" will only scare them more and elongate their sales cycle. Guide them like a teacher or counselor would do. Give them the direction they crave and desperately need!

4) Affirm them! When they give you their reason for not buying or selling now, agree with their reasoning! This makes them feel heard. Use phrases such as, "I'm sure you aren't looking to buy or sell anytime soon." They need you to de-escalate the conversation so they can think rationally versus emotionally.

Phrases and questions to use with a Dreamer:

1) Whenever you do move, what are you hoping to change about where you live?

2) Have you been looking for a home long?

3) If we could fast-forward to a year from now and you and I were talking about your home purchase, what would the perfect scenario look like for you? What would enable you to say something like, "Yes, this real estate purchase worked out great!"?

Once you've correctly assessed the individual on the phone as being a Dreamer, the real sale that needs to be made is helping the person you're speaking with transition to becoming a Planner.

If you're able to appropriately engage someone who is dreaming about buying or selling a home, you can help them feel comfortable enough to use you as a resource. When this happens, they begin asking you questions about the process overall and what they should be doing now. If you sense this shift in the conversation or relationship, you've likely transitioned them into the planning or preparation phase.

I believe an argument could be made that the transition from a Dreamer to a Planner is a vital skill that must be learned if an agent wants to be able to produce a high volume of sales in the future. Other large advertising companies have more market share and are able to obtain the information of the people who are urgently shopping for a home. It's hard to compete with their billion-dollar marketing budgets. If we don't learn how to go after a different type of lead and learn to convert it, the large players will squeeze you out of the market.

The thing to remember about the transition of a Dreamer to a Planner is that something about the call with you—the conversation, the content shared, the rapport established, the overall feeling you've given them—has caused the person to trust you enough to start asking questions. Once you've become a source of valuable information for the prospect, the likelihood of becoming that person's agent is very high. You'll need to listen to the person you're speaking with to see if they are looking to become more serious right away or if they need more time.

Characteristics of a Planner:

1) Once Planners trust the agent as a valuable information source, they will typically work with that agent exclusively.

2) The Planner isn't typically swayed by an agent just saying something such as, "I'm valuable" or "I know a lot, so you should listen to me." The Planner will follow the agent who shows their value and demonstrates their knowledge.

3) The Planner needs to feel calm and without pressure to learn something new. While this doesn't mean you aren't still trying to close the lead, it does mean you use extra care to nudge the person along.

Adapting to the Planner:

1) Scratch their itch. Start with teaching them about topics that interest them. Whether it's interest out of fear of messing up or interest out of enjoyment, start with teaching them what they want to learn. You'll learn what they want to know more about based on their questions.

2) Try to share information they aren't likely to know. We try to discuss financing, appraisal requirements, loan approval requirements, and process—anything that is hard to read about online.

Phrases and questions to use with a Planner:

1). "What's the plan?" This sounds funny, but it works. Get right to it so they can tell you either that they don't have one or they have a bad one that they probably won't actually follow through on. Either way, this is a win for you!

2) "Have you thought about [insert minor details that they likely haven't thought of]?" Examples of "thoughts" would be: money involved, investment potential, and crime ratings.

Next up are categories three and four: the Shoppers and Transactors. I'm going to tackle these last two together, because in both of these instances, you're dealing with someone who has figured out a specific need and wants some help.

As agents, we love these types of leads. We are able to shut off our brain and be told what to do. I'm not saying salespeople who enjoy this type of lead are somehow less skilled or less hardworking. Personally, I love these types of leads because it takes less effort. When an agent is looking for a new lead source, they want a lead source that produces this kind of lead: someone who knows what they want and wants you to help them obtain it.

The challenges with building your business from this type of lead are: 1) There aren't many of these leads to go around, 2) they are very expensive, and 3) we can't control the readiness of the consumer to buy or sell when we talk to them. While we can be excited when we speak to someone who is ready to buy a home right away, we shouldn't *depend* on this type of lead. This is why the first two categories are important to understand.

If a salesperson can adapt quickly on the phone, they can be relevant to both the Shoppers and Transactors and the Dreamers who are not at all ready to transact leads. Your success with any of these prospect categories depends on your ability to listen and follow what you're hearing with the right questions.

My wife and I foster children for the city of Virginia Beach, VA, along with raising our own biological children. The city requested that we do play-based therapy with one of the children to help learn about and manage her behavior. The child was only four years old, yet she had experienced much trauma and had a significant amount of behavioral challenges. I bring this up because one of the statements by the therapists always stood out to me. As we were framing the playtime, they told me that I was not allowed to ask any questions and I was to follow the child's lead with play.

The therapist went on to say, "Questions control the conversation because you're dictating what is being played with. Simply follow their lead." Perhaps it was because I was working on this chapter at the time, but questions controlling the conversation really stood out to me because that is what we emphasize on our team: utilizing questions to lead the consumer down the path we are wanting them to go. We do this simply because we know more than they do, and they need our leadership.

Actionable Takeaways in This Chapter:

Know the four categories of home buyers and sellers: Dreamers, Planners, Shoppers, and Transactors.

Adjust your approach to provide the right kind of value to each.

Don't waste your time, money, or energy waiting for the Planners, Shoppers, or Transactors to fall in your lap.

7.

THE SOCRATIC METHOD
OF SELLING

HERE'S A FUN fact about me: I have several degrees, two of which are in theology and ministry. I also pastored a church for ten years, from the ages of twenty to thirty years old. During my years of being a pastor, I sold real estate to support my efforts at the local church. *Wait!* Don't close the book now. Ha ha! The ministry training helped me study some of the greatest teachers ever to walk our planet. In many ways, my ministerial training helped me hone my craft of teaching, verbalizing my thoughts, and planning out a logical flow to a topic.

Unsurprisingly, the teachings of Jesus were a major focal point of my study. Setting aside whether you believe Jesus is the Son of God or not, the man named Jesus was an amazing teacher! He was very much in touch with the people, who listened to him, and he was always able to evoke sincere thought as he taught.

While studying his approach to relaying information, I discovered he used an approach similar to the philosopher Socrates. I searched for the phrase "Socratic method of teaching" and found the following definition on Wikipedia:

> *The basic form of the Socratic method is a series of questions formulated as tests of logic and fact intended to help a person or group discover their beliefs about some topic, explore definitions, and seek to characterize general characteristics shared by various particular instances.*

While studying Jesus's teaching, I understood this approach to teaching as asking questions that led the person to think critically about a subject. I then, of course, thought I was innovating a new idea and thought I invented the idea of Socratic selling.

Unfortunately for me, it was already a well-established topic by the 1980s, so I can't take credit for it. However, I certainly subscribe to the approach! This is how I taught when I would preach a sermon. I wouldn't make assumptions, but rather I would aim to find common ground with the churchgoers and help them see the reality of where they were and the truth I was attempting to provide them with. The more I dove into this approach, the more success I had in ministry. At the age of twenty-two, I was traveling the country preaching for a week at a time to churches that would have me. (Yes, I was a traveling evangelist, and it was a great way to see different parts of the country!)

This dual career of ministry and real estate helped me see the buying journey from multiple perspectives. When I started to focus on online lead generation around 2011, I realized most of the people I spoke with had no idea where to start with buying a home. While I didn't want to push them into buying or selling, I also felt that if I didn't try to help them at that very moment, I was doing them a disservice. In many ways, I was serving the person on the other end of the phone by being a real estate evangelist. Yes, I just made that title up, but that's essentially what I was.

Armed with my real estate sermons (another made-up title), I would end up working with eight out of ten prospects with who I had a conversation—that's 80 percent for you math buffs! The conversion percentages were off-the-charts amazing. I wasn't even paying attention, nor did I even know what a conversion percentage was at the time, but I was absolutely crushing it.

I am going to share the exact questions and cadence I used to convert such a high number of prospects into clients. However, before I give you a "script" to work from, I need to ensure that your mindset is in the right place. There are three areas of mindset that you must get clear about in order for this to work.

Mindset Principle #1

It's not about you. Or your paycheck. Come from a place of sincerity and a passion to help people. You can have the best questions or scripts in the world, but people remember 90 percent of how you made them feel and 10 percent of what you said. They'll remember the feelings before they remember the words. Being authentically passionate about helping them is incredibly important.

Mindset Principle #2

If you are anxious, worried, or concerned that they will not like or enjoy your help, you are focused on the wrong person. You should be thinking about the person you're supposed to be advising. When you're timid or shy, you're focused on how *you* have a concern or problem. **You must stop focusing on yourself and focus on the person on the other end of the phone.** This person is preparing to make the largest financial transaction of their life. The less *you*-focused you become, the more your conversion numbers will skyrocket. Being people-focused instead of self-focused helps you to authentically come from a place of contribution.

I recently had to purchase a larger vehicle to make room for our growing family. I started speaking with two different salespeople at two different dealerships early on a Friday. That evening, someone in my family had a heart attack. Needless to say, it wasn't going to be a good weekend to buy a new car. My extended family needed help, and my wife and I were really focused on this legitimate need. On Saturday, the two dealerships reached out to try and close the sale. I told both salespeople the same thing: "This isn't a good weekend to buy a car due to a family emergency." Both salespeople were incredibly nice and understanding. There was one main difference, however. Salesperson A was kind and sympathetic and just told me that we could reconnect the following week. I was grateful she made it easy on me and quickly hung up the phone. Salesperson B was similarly sympathetic and advised me that there was no rush to buy. However, salesperson B also added that he could check to see if he could keep the larger car over the weekend to give more wiggle room for the family as we went around town, and we could buy the car a few days later.

Both salespeople were nice, responsive, and caring. However, Salesperson B obtained my business because he was aggressively helpful and added value to my purchase.

Mindset Principle #3

Be curious in an endearing way. We have all spoken to someone who will ask a question but doesn't listen to the answer. In a general sense, men seem to have more trouble in this area than women. Just ask my wife! However, everyone deals with this lack of care and focus in some capacity. When you're speaking to someone, if you are curious to know more, it will show your sincerity and advance the conversation. Think about the last time you were speaking to someone about something you found important to you. For example, my wife is an excellent listener! I love it when she has the time to listen to me blab about work. I know she doesn't really care about business dealings, but because she cares about me, she listens. Where it gets very exciting for me is when she will ask a question that makes it seem like she wants to know more about the subject.

Example:

Me: "Wow, honey! I ran a new type of Facebook ad and the CPL [cost per lead] is only $2.00!"

Her: "That's great! What do you think was different about the ad?"

Now, I know marketing doesn't interest her, and CPL isn't something she's thrilled to discuss. However, when she asks what's different about the ad, it lets me dive deep with her in a way that makes me feel understood.

Just like Dale Carnegie would tell us a prospect's favorite word in the English language is their own name, someone who is talking about themselves loves to hear the person they are talking with seem interested in what they are saying. There is no better way to do this than to decide to be sincerely interested in what they are saying.

Being curious and asking follow-up questions to a prospect is a great way to also handle objections from them. If they say something such as, "I can't buy a home until I save up enough money," you can say something such as, "I understand. It's great you are setting money aside. Just curious, where did you find out how much money you needed to save?" As you can see, handling objections in a way that brings the person close with compliments and then probing for more info is an incredible way to build rapport and advance the conversation.

By having the mindset of a sincere and passionate teacher, by being focused on the other person and not yourself, and last, by deciding to be someone who is curious about the person they are talking with, the following questions will absolutely crush your lead follow-up. I came upon this mindset and these questions organically, not realizing they would be so effective, but they have consistently kept my lead conversion to eight or nine out of every ten conversations I had.

Key questions to help you teach the prospect:

Question 1: Search Criteria: What are you hoping to change about where you live when you do end up moving?

Question 2: Financing: Do you happen to have a friend in the real estate business?

We only ask this question to bring the financing discussion up. Regardless of whether the prospect says yes or no, we begin the dialogue by discussing how important it is to deal with the financial topic early on.

Question 3: Planning: What would be the perfect scenario with regards to your home purchase?

Question 4: Have you signed anything that requires you to only work with one agent?

Actionable Takeaways in This Chapter:

Remember, it's not about you. Push your insecurities to the side so you can focus on being an active listener and an aggressive helper.

Curiosity is a choice. Decide to be interested, and you'll automatically have more natural conversations.

8.

WANT TO STAND OUT? ACT LIKE YOU CARE

I BRIEFLY TOUCHED on this experience in the last chapter, but it's worth delving into a little deeper. In 2019 my wife and I decided that, via foster care, we wanted to try to help children in our area who were without a home or were in the guardianship of the city. There was an increased need due to drug addiction, and we wanted to try and help out. We spent months preparing in classes and home studies, and emotionally preparing ourselves and our own children for some changes.

One of the changes we had to make was taking my small sedan and trading it for a large three-row vehicle. I felt I wanted a minivan, but I just couldn't buy into the image. (Don't judge me; I couldn't help it!)

We finally decided to take a look at a Chevy Tahoe. I liked it because it had a great mixture of both style and size. As mentioned, the same weekend we went to look for a new vehicle, a member of our family suffered a heart attack. From extending our family to extending our vehicle to supporting a family member in the hospital, it was a challenging time! We chose to purchase the Tahoe from the salesperson, who went the extra mile to make this stressful time a little easier. Simply put, he cared.

When I think of standing out as a salesperson in real estate, I am reminded of my "go-to" approach for calling homeowners of expired, withdrawn, and for sale by owner listings. Most agents call these prospects often using a number of tactics, attempting to stand out. Some agents go with the egotistical approach of, "I sell a million homes a year," while others use the relational approach of something similar to, "Oh, I think our kids went to the same school!" Neither of which ever really appealed to me because that wasn't who I was.

Authenticity is an important trait to remember when attempting to stand out. It is my opinion that most top performers have found a way to be an authentic version of who they believe they are. Whether they are genuine or not isn't the point of this chapter; top salespeople represent themselves in an authentic way, which resonates deeply with people. Standing out just to stand out will never be as effective as standing out while still being your true self. So when I was regularly calling expired sellers, I would always come at it from a legitimate desire to help them.

Many times the reason their home did not sell was due to simple mistakes by the listing agent that could easily be corrected if they decided to relist their home. I would simply tell the people what I thought they should do over the phone. I called it a "free consult" to help them, regardless of whether they decided to list their home with me or not.

I can't tell you the number of times prospects on the other end of the phone would say something like, "Out of all of the agents we spoke with, you stood out because what we heard from you was so different from the rest!" My ability to stand out on the phone was not a result of my stellar sales skills; it was simply due to my desire to help from the very start of the conversation. By teaching the prospect industry secrets, I was adding value in a way that others didn't. It also made the dynamic of the relationship different because the prospect was left with a feeling of, "What else does this agent know that I and the other agents I've talked to don't?"

How to Care More (and Show It)

1) Always identify with the prospect's reason for not needing you right now. Make them feel both heard and affirmed in their reasoning for not being ready.

Remember, most prospects don't know what they're looking for yet. So when we try to create urgency, they often feel like we are too aggressive in our approach. If you speak to a prospect and they say, "I'm waiting to buy after I get my tax return," don't pressure them to make a decision now. Instead, tell them how responsible you think they are and let them know that you love working with buyers like them. If they say, "I'm just looking right now," affirm them by saying something such as, "My wife and I love looking too! It's so fun to browse different types of homes. What are you hoping to change one day about where you live right now?" Again, make the prospect feel understood, but keep the conversation focused on their future home purchase process in a way that feels easy and friendly.

2) While affirming their concern, remember that you're looking for ways to help the prospect by teaching them things they don't know. In the previous tip, I gave the example of affirming the prospect's reason for not needing help, but then I transitioned the conversation to what the person is hoping to change about where they live. By redirecting the objection to a discussion of what they hope to change about their current home, I am helping the person by giving them direction on how to think about the home-buying process. If we don't understand this point, we become the prospect's "fake friend" for the remainder of the call. You talk about many things that are

not related to their real estate needs. Even the best-intentioned salespeople can get sucked into this trap. You don't want to push or bother someone, so you overcompensate by falling into the trap of fake rapport-building

Anyone can be nice. Only a true real estate professional can add value to the real estate transaction. I enjoy building rapport while discussing a person's real estate needs. If the prospect says they are looking for a home with a large yard, I share how I like large yards as well and then offer my reason why. I might say something such as, "Oh, definitely! I love a large yard as well. I have lots of kids and a dog. One of my favorite things to do is to enjoy time with them in the backyard. Why do you, Mr. Buyer, want a large yard?" In this discussion, I've been able to focus on the area where I am valuable to the person I'm attempting to connect with while also focusing on their need for assistance.

3) At some point after implementing tips 1 and 2, you need to transition to taking control of the

conversation and act like they need your help—because if they have a real estate need, then they do need your guidance! An example of this would be similar to what we discussed in the last two tips. If you can help them feel at ease, they are more likely to be open to discussing where they are in the home-buying process. Attempt to use consultative verbiage to reflect that you have a good understanding of the direction in which the prospect needs to go.

Use phrases such as "In my professional opinion" or "In my experience, my clients have typically done X." By simply stating your role as a professional and giving direction, you are showing yourself to be knowledgeable. If we've affirmed their objection in tip 1 and started to share information the prospect likely doesn't know in tip 2, then driving the conversation the direction you need it to go in should be effortless.

The prospect feels heard; they've learned something. Now you're ready to lead them. Most real estate agents are waiting for the lead's need for real estate to define the next steps. This is a big part of why so many agents only sell two to three homes a year. Rather than leading the person into what will most likely be the largest purchase of their life, we are waiting for them to figure it out on their own and tell us when they are ready. Are you starting to catch a glimpse of how much we cheapen our role in their purchase? Rather than driving the process like a true guide or counselor, we relegate our role to a waiter or waitress. We are waiting for them to tell us their "order" for their real estate purchase. Do they want a three-bedroom? We get them a three-bedroom. Do they want a steak? We ask, "Medium or rare?" We ask, "Medium or rare?" While being a food server is an honorable way to earn a living, it's not what we've been licensed to do. We've been licensed to help folks buy and sell real estate. Anything outside of this role is below our trade.

Actionable Takeaways in This Chapter:

Identify and affirm their reason for not being ready.

While affirming, teach them something they don't know (show your value).

Take control of the conversation and show them why they need your help.

9.

LEARNING TO SAY NO SO YOUR BUSINESS CAN THRYVE!

THE CHALLENGE WITH being a nice person is that people equate being nice with being weak. If you recall, my DISC profile test indicated that I should just be a big teddy bear helping people so that they would like me. The desire to please people has always been such a strong motivator for me. As a pastor, this was insanely difficult for me because the congregation needed to follow me, like me, pay me, and respect me. I remember just walking around trying to ensure everyone was upbeat and happy because then I felt like I was doing a good job. As a single, unmarried, childless man, I could navigate this easily because whoever was in front of me was my priority. However, as new people came into my life, mainly my wife and children, allowing the person in front of me to be the priority became a huge issue. Thankfully, my wife has the patience of a saint.

As a full-time real estate agent over the last twenty years, allowing my clients to be the priority was always my standard practice. Whichever client had my attention, I was consumed with their needs and wants. While that sounds honorable, the issue for me was it also meant that whatever client or clients I had were driving my schedule. This did pay my bills, but there was no long-term goal in mind of what I wanted to obtain in my career. A decade went by, and I was still on the hamster wheel of trying to find new business every month and trying to close it. If I'm being candid, my business was relegated to luck, and as you know, my luck ran out during the crash of 2008.

When an agent allows his or her clients to run the show, there is no big-picture direction. I call it the tyranny of the urgent. Whatever is urgent and in front of you, you focus on. This is why agents have big ups and big downs regularly. They'll have a few transactions ratified and waiting to close, and instead of continuing to find and service new opportunities, they get focused on transaction-specific tasks. Things such as compliance and paperwork, scheduling inspections, condo association issues, and septic tank inspections. All these things sidetrack the agent from growing their business. As such, their business dips the following few months.

Let's look at another industry and compare this scenario of the average real estate agent via a short parable:

Once, I met a farmer who was very disappointed in the lack of crops for the season. He didn't have anything to eat or sell, and he wasn't sure how he was going to make it through the season.

I became very curious, and I asked the farmer, "How did this happen? You had such a successful business."

The farmer reluctantly told me, "I became so busy chopping down my crops and packaging them, strapping and selling them at the local stores, that alas, I didn't have time to plant new crops. Now I don't have anything growing for next season. I would think about planting my seeds for next season, but by the time I got home from cutting down and packaging my crops that were already grown, I was too tired to plant new seeds.

"On a bright note, however, I have done a good job getting the food prepared that already grew last season! I took extra care chopping the crops, selling and shipping them off. While I don't have any crops ready for next year and I will likely lack money and produce next year, I used extra packaging and tape to make sure all the produce from this season had been done incredibly well. Everyone remarked how last season's crops looked so nice in the packaging. I also spoke with my other farmer friends, and we are concerned about the farming industry as a whole. Everyone is so focused on next season that they don't pack as well as we do. I just wish I had something to sell next season too. Yes, everything was well packaged last season and looked great; however, now I will go out of business for lack of crops this season."

Does this seem as silly to you as it does to me? A farmer, who should always ensure there is food on the table, was so focused on packaging his crops from last season that he forgot to plant the seeds for the next one. As real estate agents, we often find ourselves in this farmer's situation. Whether we admit it or not, we can relate to this feast-or-famine lifestyle. We're doing well for a few months, then incredibly poorly for the next month. And so the cycle goes. When everything is going right, we feel amazing (and we usually spend money like crazy). We buy leads and sign up for lead-generation platforms, CRMs, and branding ads. But when the business dries up, we are back to feeling desperate and financially strapped. It's both horrible and frustrating. But what if we can break that cycle by planting seeds every month?

To put it simply, we should never forget how important the concept of sowing and reaping is, especially in real estate and other sales-related businesses. Your success is not dependent on luck or good fortune. You can make a decision to plant new seeds daily and monthly and escape the farmer's vicious cycle.

Like the farmer who needs to cut down the crops and prepare the seeds for the next season, I told my agents I wanted them to time-block part of their day to do the things that are necessary for their business to process the transactions. The key is to separate the time to work on their business and the time to plant seeds for the months ahead. If they didn't, the coming spring would certainly be a disaster.

I told my team that by planting seeds and preparing to do what's needed for the following months, we could establish a cycle of success. This way, we won't find ourselves in a situation where we don't have any business to prospect.

So how should you prepare for this cycle of success? One thing should be clear: It isn't something relegated to luck. In real estate terms, it's not about getting a significant lead, then finding out that the lead is ready to buy a home right away this very afternoon.

Because no matter how much we love those leads, there's no way we can control the readiness of a prospect to buy a home or any product. The best thing we can do is dedicate time to be relevant to the people in our database. It's about more than grabbing the right script, uttering the right words, using the right technology, sharing a cool video, or even running a certain type of advertisement.

When we've got a group of people who we think are interested in the product we're selling—whether it's real estate, a brand-new car, or anything else—all we need to do is to stay on top of their focus as they journey through. They need to know that we are with them wherever they are in their journey. You just have to block off sections of your day to focus on what needs to be done to plant the seeds for the following months. There are many ways for you to do this, and the possibilities are endless.

If you expect to find yourself getting busier as the day goes on, and you know it's going to become more difficult to do the prospecting daily to plant seeds for your success, you need to start your day getting your prospecting out of the way. Begin your day by focusing on the duties that you think are the most challenging because that's when your brain is still fresh. You've just had your cup of coffee, so you're fired up. You haven't been yelled at by people and you're still excited about all of the possibilities the new day will bring.

With the creative fire in your belly burning brightly early in the morning, try to do the things you need to do to further your success.

Step One: Start your day with the duties that you need to get done to sow your seeds toward success. For our team, this starts by doing a set block of time prospecting inside of our CRM Follow Up Boss. Remember, when you say yes to one thing in your schedule, you are effectively saying no to something else during that time slot. Make sure you are saying yes to the right things! You can still be nice and say no. I would just offer a different time and say I was tied up at that specific time and ask if they could do a different time for the appointment. If they couldn't, then I would give in. But I would at least try to move the appointment to accommodate my schedule.

Step Two: Set long-term goals for yourself and then break them down into quarterly, monthly, weekly, and daily goals. Try to visualize your end goal. What do you need to do if you want to make $120,000 a year? If it's $10,000 a month, how many appointments and closings do you need to be able to achieve that goal?

Let's say you need to make twenty appointments a month to make $120,000 in a year. That's five appointments a week. You need to meet with twenty people to sell your product, and out of those twenty people, you need at least four of them to buy, assuming a $2,500 commission each month.

How many calls do you need to make to accomplish those five appointments? While it is different for everyone, it is best to have at least fifty. At least fifty calls will get you five appointments. At least two hundred calls a month will get you twenty set meetings. And twenty appointments will get you four closings. Four closings in a month will earn $10,000 dollars, which will give you $120,000 a year.

Accomplishing that goal of $120,000 in a year is definitely not luck. It's about daily, focused activities. As you read the next chapters of this book, I want you to be encouraged that you can make it happen in your business so that the feast and famine you had before will no longer be your experience. The choice is yours to make. But I can hear some of you say, "What does this have to do with being too nice of a salesperson?" Everything! I always wanted to please the client in front of me and I let them dictate my day-to-day. I would pat myself on the back because I pleased them, and that's all that mattered at the time. Now I realize that having boundaries means sometimes I tell my client *no*! Sometimes, for the benefit of my family and business, I need to not do what the person in front of me wants and tell them no.

Saying no to your client will allow you to have structure around your schedule so you can do more than just react to emergencies, but now you can plan your day and have a bigger goal in mind. I would recommend using a script similar to this one when you tell your client no:

The scenario is that they want to see a house Saturday at 10:00 a.m. "Hey, John! Yes, 123 Smith St. is available, so we can look at it this weekend. I do have something personal scheduled in the morning on Saturday, but I definitely want to get you in the property. Are you, by chance, available Sunday afternoon?"

This approach allows you to plan your day, but you're also not being rude to your client. Most of my clients would not have an issue with moving the day, and in the off chance your client does have an issue with moving the appointment, then give them what they want. The key here is that you want the client dictating the appointment to be the exception to the rule instead of standard operating procedure.

Actionable Takeaways in This Chapter:

Remember to plant seeds today for tomorrow's closings.

Start your day with prospecting—every day. No exceptions.

Reverse-engineer your goals into daily power tasks.

Say no sometimes to take back control of your schedule.

10.

Don't Be Annoying; Be Helpful!

The conventional wisdom of real estate agents over the last ten to twenty years was that when you obtain a lead, you follow up with that lead for months and years. The thought was that as long as the agent is checking in regularly, when the buyer is ready to buy, they will remember the agent. I'm not sure we realize this, but checking on someone over the course of two to three years to see if they are ready to buy your product is very annoying.

Running your business this way is the epitome of being self-interested. Rather than making the decision to pour into the person with information, research, advice, and guidance, the salesperson is just checking to see if they're ready. If you're being honest with yourself, the only reason you are checking in with the prospect is because you want to be there when they're ready to make a sale. But other than the desire to sell the person a house, you aren't providing anything that makes the process easier for the potential buyer or seller.

Instead of using this approach, I decided I would just try to give *so* much information to the prospect while on the phone that they had to value speaking with me again the next time I called. After all, we all love speaking with someone who provides so much insight and direction. We actually feel smarter when we hang up the phone.

You will know that providing value is an issue in your conversations when you are consistently having substantive conversations with prospects that go nowhere.

I remember years ago I had a Kutco knife salesman use the pitch of, "I just need a demo to get college credit. You don't need to buy a knife, but I need to do X amount of product demos. Let me know when we can meet." I'm not proud of this, but that guy called me at least twenty times over three weeks, and I never answered.

I actually changed the contact in my phone to "Don't answer knife guy."

The knife guy's pitch was all about *his* earning college credits and not *my* time being wasted. Whatever you do, don't become the knife guy to your prospects. You think the conversation went great, but the person never answers the phone again. The prospect is dodging your calls, not returning voicemails or texts, because when they see your number on their caller ID, they don't value the conversation enough to answer or respond.

Part of my day-to-day duties in both running my real estate teams and in my position as head realtor in residence at Ylopo is coming up with drip emails, texts, and voicemails. I believe one reason my content has become popular is because I write the material based on what I believe I would want to see if I was a buyer or seller. Some examples of this would be:

"I saw a home you might like near 123 Smith St. Would you like me to text or email it?" Or, "Afternoon, John! I saw a blog article on home buying that I thought might be helpful for you. Would you mind if I gave it to you?"

In these drips, I'm focused on giving something to my prospect. Notice that I am not asking if they found any homes they like or if they want me to send them some homes. I've based my approach on what I believe the prospect's needs are based on *their* journey instead of focusing on building out *my* pipeline.

I firmly believe that when I am sending blog articles, e-guides, infographics, and other content, 99 percent of the people I send them to don't actually read the content. Luckily, I'm not sending it so they read it. I'm sending valuable content because I want them to remember me as an agent who sends valuable content.

Checking on a prospect in your database becomes effortless when you're sending content to them, because you can just mention their search without making it the focus of the conversation. For example, instead of asking if the prospect has found a home, you can ask if they would like you to send the item of value and/or if they've received the item of value that you already sent them. As you're focused on the item of value, just plainly say something to the effect of, "While I have you, how's the search coming along?" I have found that this is the most effortless and organic way to check on a prospect's buying or selling journey without pushing them away.

Another way in which an agent can be helpful (not annoying) is to help the prospect down the path of self-discovery. We've already reviewed the Socratic method of questions and how the questions teach the person how to think about a subject. However, there is another dimension to this section that will help the prospect find comfort by talking with you:

You want to slip into the role of counselor and guide.

Have you ever been to therapy? My wife and I did a few marriage checkup therapy sessions a few years ago. I'm not naturally gifted with being self-aware or even knowing what I want. But I can still remember the first time we walked out of the therapist's office. I was so excited! Speaking with someone who helped me figure out what I think or how I feel was an amazing feeling.

The funny thing about it was the therapy session was less about them fixing my issues and more about asking me questions about what I thought. When I would answer the therapist's question, the therapist would stay focused on my reply and want to continue to go deeper.

After answering the therapist's questions, she would then say, "And how did you come to that conclusion?" or "That's interesting. Why is that?" She would also say things such as, "OK, I see where you are coming from on that. Tell me more about how you learned to respond in this way." A good therapist asks her questions to help the person receiving the counseling clear the fog and dig deep to find out what's making them anxious.

If the therapist's approach to the discussion were to be our gold standard as agents, then you can see that just calling a lead and asking something lame such as, "Did you see a home?" or "Have you been preapproved yet?" is a terrible approach. There's no value to the prospect. It's all about the agent checking off a box. The people who don't think they need you but have a long-term real estate goal are where massive ROI is found.

I recommend writing down four to five general items of value a potential prospect would appreciate from you so that you can pull them out at a moment's notice. The truth of the matter is that people aren't really focused on the item of value you're providing. It just feels good to know you're working with a professional who wants to be supportive. This approach is so dramatically different from what your competitors are doing that it will attract business to you.

We do our best to utilize a coming-from-giving attitude with every aspect of our business. One area we've used this approach on is with FSBO and/or expired listings. Rather than trying to tell the person how amazing we are and how we market real estate better than others, we provide an over-the-phone consult on two to three things they can do to either sell their home on their own or that they could teach their agent with. We tell the homeowner that we have a "secret" plan to give them some killer secrets to get their home sold so that they will either a) realize how awesome we are or b) be so impressed with our advice that they will tell their friends about us. We list a lot of homes with this approach.

Actionable Takeaways in This Chapter:

Give, give, give to the prospect. And make sure this works into your drips and conversations.

Become a guide or a counselor who gives the client the direction they need.

Be focused on the client, not yourself, and you'll connect with more prospects.

11.

THE EVER-ELUSIVE SELLER LEADS AND HOW TO CONVERT THEM!

I'M GOING TO let you in on a little secret. Homeowners don't like talking about selling their home. No really, they don't. At. All.

The only person who enjoys talking about selling a home is a real estate agent or investor. This dichotomy is so severe that it causes most real estate agents to be completely out of touch when attempting to generate and convert a seller lead.

The typical conversation goes something like this:

Agent: "Hi, John? This is Barry over at Better Homes and Gardens Real Estate. I was giving you a call because I saw you were interested in finding out more about your home value."

Seller: "Yes, I was able to get the info. Thanks for your time, but we don't need any additional help."

Agent: Oh, OK. The market is really great right now, so I wanted to see if you were open to selling anytime soon?"

Seller: "No, I just wanted the report. Thanks again."

Click.

The issue in the preceding scenario is the agent is focused on what he wants to talk about versus being in touch with the homeowner and their lack of desire to discuss selling their home. Rather than focusing on what the homeowner wants to focus on, and the homeowner's disdain for discussing selling their home, the agent just went right to it. This, in principle, is why many agents never convert seller leads.

Let's compare this to another approach:

Agent: "Hi, John? This is Barry over at Better Homes and Gardens Real Estate. I was just giving you a call because I saw you asked for a report on your home value. I wanted to make sure the report landed in your inbox and not your spam."

Seller: "Yes, I received that report and was able to open it. Thank you."

Agent: "Oh, great. Did you have any questions concerning the information?"

Seller: "No, it was pretty straightforward."

Agent: "OK, great! I also have [insert item of value] that could give additional information. Would you like me to text or email that?"

Seller: "Email is fine. Thank you."

Agent: "Sure, no problem. I'm sure you didn't wake up today thinking to yourself, 'I think I'm going to sell my home tomorrow' or anything crazy like that, but I'm curious about something. I have a few buyers looking for a home like yours, and I was curious, if someone wanted to offer a very high amount of money for your home, would you be open to the discussion in the next six to twelve months?"

While the preceding script revision isn't foolproof, you will find a conversation like this will be more effective because it eases the prospect into the topic and doesn't get right to it. This revision also offers items of value that the seller appreciates versus just asking for the business. By recognizing the homeowner doesn't want to talk about selling first, the agent is much more likely to engage the prospect.

We have found tremendous success with setting a pre-listing appointment with a homeowner versus setting the typical "I'd love to see your home" or "We can start planning" approaches/scripts. Our pre-listing appointment process is to help the homeowner understand what buyers are expecting to see in a home condition-wise in the current market. If it's a seller's market, we walk the home and help them see they don't have many repairs that need to be done. This is always very good news for a homeowner and likely will speed them up. In a buyer's market, we will help the homeowner prioritize repairs to ensure they are spending money on the key repairs to procure a buyer.

As you can see, the pre-listing strategy is very consistent with the previous script revisions in that it is setting an appointment for something that the homeowner perceives to be valuable today. The appointment is not for the agent; it's for the seller. This is dramatically different than the agent who sets an appointment only to get to know the client. We both know you want to get to know the seller for your own business growth. The seller doesn't need any more friends. However, setting an appointment to decrease the workload and stress of the homeowner is invaluable. We have found that homeowners overwhelmingly feel a sense of release when they realize that in a seller's market, they don't have to fix much. Preparing the home to sell is often a big blocker to someone wanting to list their home. Remember, the homeowner knows their home very well and knows every crack, squeaky floor, leaking pipe, and missing shingle. The list can be daunting and expensive. When we've been able to decrease this list in both length and cost, the homeowner lists much faster.

Thus far in this, we've really been focused on new seller leads, or seller leads that are considering selling right now. There is another element to your seller lead conversion that I want to mention that involves a longer-term nurture process that doesn't depend on you being persistent (read: annoying) and in front of the person on your own for years.

As I've mentioned before, everyone who owns a home is interested in what the value is. Checking your home value doesn't make you a seller lead. It makes you a homeowner who is interested in their value. While real estate agents want seller leads that have a sense of urgency, the real money is in the people who aren't quite ready yet. If you can keep your brand in front of the homeowner via some kind of social media or email strategy that isn't annoying, you can be memorable. Further, if you can send valuable content such as in-depth automated reports and/or informative blogs or articles, you can send the info and sit back and observe the consumer's behavior to respond accordingly.

My role at Ylopo has had me obsessing over seller leads and seller nurture for over a year. Being able to partner with one of the great marketing minds of our generation, Jeufeng Ge, has been an eye-opening experience for the power and relevance digital marketing has in the real estate space. As Ge—as the Ylopo team calls him—and I have dug deep on this topic of seller lead nurture, I've found three specific things that homeowners want to know more about:

1) How much equity they have

2) How the local market is doing and what that means for them

3) If there are buyers looking for a home like theirs

Notice that none of the preceding three things have anything to do with how long you've been an agent, that your dog Pookie is really fun, or how many platinum awards your broker gave you for selling more than the other agents in your office. The homeowner who doesn't know you personally could care less about you right now. It's all about their home and how it's likely the largest financial investment of their lives. When your marketing ads, emails, drip campaigns, and content creation are focused on the seller's interests, it's instantly more effective.

When your technology setup allows you to automatically monitor the homeowners in your database to see activity, you're able to talk to the right person, at the right time, with the right message. When I wrote the messaging for Ylopo's Raiya system, I went deep on this for seller lead nurture. Raiya doesn't text the homeowner one hundred different ways of saying, "Do you want to sell?" Raiya comes from value and makes sure the data requested landed in the person's inbox; she offers reports, lists of buyers, local market data, and many other helpful tips. Eventually, believe it or not, she stops talking about the homeowner's home and their desire to sell. She shifts to discussing the buying journey. This is because discussing what home the homeowner will buy next is typically something they would enjoy talking about. The lead engagement of the scripts I've worked on with Ylopo for Raiya has had higher engagement than anything else the artificial intelligence team has ever seen. I strongly believe it's due to Raiya's ability to be relevant.

I cannot overstate the value of having a technology setup of a CRM, digital marketing system integrated, and remarketing technology to bring leads back to your website. I was just in a meeting with several members of the Ylopo team discussing what I would do if I needed to find good seller leads in my CRM. I'm sharing this here because I believe it is a great example of why these things matter:

Search Criteria in My CRM Follow-Up Boss:

1) Home Address is not an empty field (aka I have their home address)

2) Last site visit in the last thirty days (recently active)

3) Any of the following Tags: YPRIORITY, HANDRAISER, AI_ENGAGED (Tags added by Ylopo signifying the lead did something important)

4) Stage: Lead or Contact (unconverted leads)

5) Revaluate score of over 80 percent (likely to move score)

The result of the preceding criteria showed me 463 people who owned their home and were recently searching on my site. They've never been converted or spoken to by an agent and are likely to move in the next twelve months. As you can see, by having a system that keeps homeowners' attention, I am able to drill down my database to find people who are deserving of my time who might be looking to sell in the next year. If you combine this type of process with my scripting and mindset in the beginning of this chapter, you will be sure to find a high volume of listings to sell!

12.

SOMETIMES THINGS DON'T WORK LIKE THEY SHOULD

MY HOPE IS that by now you've received several ideas and strategies to build your business. The real estate industry does not have a shortage of good ideas. I would argue that we have an abundance of ideas but not enough execution of those ideas. With that in mind, I want to give you some insight that as you attempt to roll out these new processes, ideas, and goals into your day-to-day, things won't always work out the way you'd hoped. Many times—actually, most times—things don't work out the way we had hoped. I shared my story in the first chapter about how the challenging events in my life taught me life principles that changed the direction of my business.

Running a business is hard. I know that, and you know that. This book might have motivated you, given you direction and ideas, and inspired you. But when things don't work out the way you want, what are you going to do to keep going? For me, it comes down to how bad you want it. Of course, we all yell, "We want it a lot!" However, do you want it enough to do the work in silence? To work when you're tired, unmotivated, or discouraged? There's beauty in consistency, and my hope for you and I is that we embrace consistency and walk it out.

I was hoping to share a personal story to close this book out. Little did I know that a doozie of a story was coming down the pipe. My wife and I brought our third child into the world in January 2021. We had been very careful with COVID protocols for most of 2020. With COVID being such an issue for almost all of 2020 and with Nicole being pregnant, she was high risk, which made us even more on edge. With all the precautions we utilized, we still ended up contracting the virus while we were at the hospital delivering the baby. We had planned on the birth of the baby being one of great joy.

This was now our third child, so we knew what to expect and had planned appropriately. I had taken the necessary time off, and we had purchased the many things a new baby will need. I felt like this would be the baby that we would finally handle perfectly. Things were perfect for approximately a week or so. We spent lots of time kissing our little baby and introducing him to his brothers. What started as a slight cough when I would carry something heavy soon became a full-on COVID wheezing that made it hard to function. My wife slowly started to contract similar symptoms. Before we knew it, we all (baby included) began exhibiting symptoms. When we stopped being able to taste food, that's when we knew the virus had taken hold. To say that month was hard is an understatement. Not only did we have long days and nights tending to our new baby and his two brothers, but we also were fighting an incredibly challenging virus.

I attempted to see if we could hire a nurse to support us as we fought the virus, but the cost was insanely high to have someone come for just a few hours a day. We were isolated in every way, and we weren't able to enjoy those early days as much as we had planned. I remember reflecting with my wife about this book during those first few days of having COVID. I felt horrible but well enough to pan out and wonder why this was occurring!

I went on to tell her that we had made it a year without contracting the virus, and here we were in one of the most vulnerable moments of our life with three children and no one allowed to come near us due to contracting the virus. I then said something along the lines of the fact that there's purpose in this pain. Before I give you the impression that I was walking confidently around happy as a clam while tending to my wife who had just delivered a baby, my week-old baby, and a house of COVID-infected family members, I'll be clear and say that I was a mess! I was feeling tired, overwhelmed, confused, frustrated, and many other negative feelings. But in the midst of feeling horrible, I didn't give up. I didn't have a choice, really. I knew my family needed me, and while I wanted to go to the hospital and be tended to, I knew that my wife and children needed my presence. So I more or less just stumbled my way through January 2021. It wasn't fast, it wasn't pretty, but I did it.

I didn't have a smile on my face often, I might have (I did) complained occasionally (a lot), but I made it through that month. Some of you have read this book with the mindset that you are going to make millions in sales effortlessly. But a few months in, you see that more often than not, people don't want to talk to you. People aren't banging down your door to sell their home. In fact, for many of you, it's hard to even have a conversation about real estate with people without them giving you the cold shoulder.

I want you to know that you are not broken, you are not a failure, and you are not worthless just because you are facing challenges in your business. I would argue that if you're not facing challenges, it's likely because you aren't doing anything. The real estate industry, more than others, tends to be made up of a guru type of culture. Everyone wants to follow the leading guru, and there's always this feeling for many that they are missing out on the secret knowledge key to wild success. While there are tips and tricks to running a successful business, at the end of the day, hard work, determination, and raw grit are what are going to help you get through the challenges you face.

When my family had COVID, I had to make a really challenging decision. I could have found relief by sitting in a hospital bed or I could have stuck it out and been there for them. I was uncomfortable.

Uncomfortable.

I don't like discomfort. I dislike it more than most, I think. Plodding through my days with COVID but still having to care for others was one of the most grueling things I've had to do. But I didn't have a choice. I *had* to get through this and I *had* to support my family. It took a month or two for all of the symptoms to leave, but we got through it.

When you start to have conversations with people in your CRM and they begin to push back and tell you they don't want help from you, can you say that you're in the place that you're going to work through being uncomfortable to realize your goals? Or are you going to quickly get off the phone because you're scared to bother the person? The choice is yours! Either make the decision to walk out the day-to-day of your business challenges or find a new career. But please, stop complaining and stop blaming everyone around you.

I could have easily called the hospital where we contracted the virus and complained. I could have posted angry posts to Facebook or been enraged at my dilemma. But instead, I decided to see what the opportunity for growth was in the midst of my challenge.

This is the pattern of the successful. It may not be pretty, it may not be easy, but it gets done. I love the old *Rocky* movies. If you've seen any of them, you know that Rocky gets pummeled in every one of the films. His face looks like a pepperoni pizza, and he can barely make out a word, but he keeps standing. Be like Rocky! Walkout these principles even if it's uncomfortable or confusing. You won't regret it. Trust me!

Appendix

MORE ABOUT MY FAITH

I WAS RECENTLY asked what my purpose in writing this book was. I had assumed the introduction explained much of this, but the question caused me to revisit the subject. I've decided to add this appendix for those wondering why my faith in Jesus Christ is essential to the foundation for much of this book and me.

I grew up in a Christian home and went to a Christian school until 5th grade, so I had some foundation of Christianity. However, in practice, I didn't follow God in any capacity. I was your typical selfish kid doing what I wanted, when I wanted. I moved out of my parents' home when I was eighteen when I purchased my first home. Around this time, I started to hang out with some kids who influenced me negatively. Much of my high school life was sheltered because I was on an elite basketball team that ended up winning the Virginia state championship and I played junior Olympic volleyball as well. My athletic life didn't give me much room to mess around. Waking up at 6:00 a.m. for practice before a full day of school or Saturday morning workouts didn't really mix well with being hungover. But my senior year, after all my seasons were over, I threw caution to the wind and started going to more parties, and being in environments that had people getting drunk, wasted, or high.

It was during this eighteenth year of my life that a few events occurred I'd like to share. One of the friends I started to spend a lot of time with was a buddy. I will call him Ace. Ace was an absolutely horrible influence on me. He was nothing short of brilliant, and rather than using his brilliant mind for school and his future occupation, he used his mind to craft schemes of theft, drugs, and other criminal activity. While I didn't involve myself with many of his schemes, there was no doubt that he was impacting my day to day in a massive way. Just by being in the car with him, I would regularly see drugs being sold, stolen property being dropped off, and all kinds of fighting. An interesting parallel during this time was that my dad was starting a church that I had zero interest in attending. The church was in a movie theater and going to church on a Sunday morning meant that I wouldn't be able to sleep in. That alone made me not interested, on top of the fact that I had no desire to change my life. My dad wanted me to go to a special event or service, so I begrudgingly went. I have no idea what he preached on or why it hit me so hard, but I felt a heavy weight of my own sin and the need to be forgiven from it. I did, in fact, give my life to Jesus that day, and it's a day I will never forget. If you thought my story would be all sunshine and rainbows now, you were wrong. While I sincerely repented of my sin and gave my life to Jesus Christ, I still had the same group of friends I was spending time with. Ace was still a day-to-day person that I was being influenced by. Ace enjoyed watching me struggle with temptation in those first few months of trying to live the Christian life. He would purposely put me in situations he knew would be difficult for me to navigate, and Ace would sit back and wait to see if I was going to give in to all the "religious nonsense," as he put it. A trip to New York was one of these hard forks in the road for me. I had been to New York twice in the last few months and was absolutely in love with the city's energy. For some reason, I was captivated by driving through the town and how there were no lanes. You could just weave in and out of cars as much as you wanted! One of the trips I remembered getting to New York at 2:00 a.m., and with not many people on the road, I was weaving through the city streets, yelling "Weeeee!" out of the window. It was so different from what I was used to, so I really liked it. There was always so much to do and see, so going on another road trip with my friends was very exciting for me. This was what made this scenario so challenging for me. I earnestly wanted to go.

I can't tell you how badly I wanted to go on this trip. My friends had booked a nice hotel, had a few restaurants they had heard of to visit, and were planning on getting back before I had to be back home. I had my conversion experience at my dad's church only a few months previously, and I was brand new to living a life devoted to the ways of God. I kept telling Ace that I would go on the trip with them until the night before. I told them I wouldn't be able to go because Jesus was very strongly convicting me that I wasn't supposed to be in the car. I didn't remember how I said it because I wasn't familiar with the word "conviction," but I knew God wasn't going to be okay with me being in that car. Of course, they laughed at me as they sped off, and I felt like a complete moron. The next few hours were dark, lonely, and sad. I felt like I made a huge mistake, and FOMO (Fear of Missing Out) was real as I went to sleep that night. My buddy Ace didn't tell me all of the details about this trip because he planned to purchase $100,000 of drugs to bring back to Virginia.

During this period of my life, I was used to talking with Ace every few days. I hadn't heard from him during the trip or several days after they were supposed to be back. After a week of silence, I started to feel like maybe I had ruined my friendship with him. I found out a few days later that Ace and two other individuals did go to New York as planned, and purchased $100,000 in drugs. But, on the way back home, they got a speeding ticket going twenty miles per hour over the speed limit.

Going this fast was considered reckless driving in our area. Something about the car was suspect to the trooper, so they searched the vehicle and found all the hidden drugs. My friends were now looking at twenty to twenty-five years in jail. I was supposed to be in that car. That problematic few days of deciding to do what God wanted me to do was the difference between my being in a jail cell or not. While Ace and the other folks in the car were having to face jail time, courts, bond hearings, and the impact of their loved ones finding out who they really were, I was living life without a care. This last-minute decision and the influence I felt God had had on that moment in my life had changed my destiny forever.

This turn of events had a significant impact on how seriously I took my faith. I felt like I was saved from a tragedy, and this compelled me to dive into the subject of God, Jesus, and the Bible. I started to feel the call to become a preacher and go to a Bible College. Bible College was interesting. My time in this academic environment could really be the subject of an entire book, as I had many highs and lows during my time spent working on my two separate degrees in ministry and theology. One of the moments I'd never forget was while I was doing one of my required ministry electives. The track I had chosen was preaching to the local prisoners in a cold jail in Rock Island, Illinois. The onboarding of my time in that ministry with the jail chaplain was very eye-opening. He told my friend and me that under no circumstances should I shake the inmates' hands due to germs/filth, take all of the staples out of the booklets we had, and when I prayed with the group of inmates, to not close my eyes due to safety concerns. And with that, he sent me down the hallway into a room of twenty to thirty inmates, with no guard or protection: just me, my Bible, and a message to share. When I was preparing for my message to the inmates, I felt very strongly during my time in prayer that every inmate in the room with me would give their life to Jesus that day. That might not sound like a profound thing, but rarely does a preacher give a message and twenty-five out of twenty-five of the listeners wholeheartedly agree with the sermon and want to radically change their life forever.

So there I was, with a firm belief that my message would be so powerful that everyone would love it. I started to share my teaching, and all of a sudden, a loud alarm went off, and the previously locked doors through the jail all opened. A few seconds later, inmates throughout the prison started changing rooms, and almost every person in my class got up and left. I asked one of the inmates what was happening and he said he didn't know. As quickly as people left, the doors locked again and there were two men left in the room. I was so disappointed because I thought I had believed the impression that everyone would give their life to Christ while in prayer. Nevertheless, I gave the same message I had planned ahead of time and decided to give it everything I had. At the end of the message, I noticed the two men that stayed in the class were crying. The message of Jesus dying for their sins and the man on the cross next to Jesus being punished for theft, and how he asked for forgiveness from Jesus rocked the inmates. They were so surprised that Jesus would so quickly give a criminal grace and mercy before dying that they realized they had hoped to. I prayed with both men, gave them a Bible, and promptly left the jail to head home. I was about halfway home when I realized that what I thought God told me actually did happen, but not the way I had planned. The impression I received in prayer was that everyone in the room would be saved, and everyone who was left in the room after the sudden disruption did receive the message of salvation. When this hit me, I was delighted that I could be a part of something like this. I never would forget the look of peace on the inmates' faces after they prayed with me that day.

A few years later, during my senior year, I was at Bible college and saw a young man who was a foreign exchange student from India. He smiled and waved. He introduced himself, and we began chatting in between classes. His family was in India, and he had to pay for college on his own. He couldn't wait to get back to India to help them win more people to Jesus. While talking with him, I noticed that 80% of his front tooth was missing. I don't typically notice people's teeth, but his tooth really stood out to me for some reason. The next day, I felt like I was supposed to give him $400 to cover the expense of his tooth being repaired. I didn't know how I came up with that number, but that's what I felt like I was supposed to do. We hadn't discussed his teeth, so I was anxious that he would be embarrassed when I told him I had the money for dental work. Later that day, I handed the cash to the young man, and he began to cry. He cried so profusely that I thought I bothered him. I had walked up to him and said, "Hello! I know this sounds crazy, but I felt like God wanted me to give you $400 to cover the cost of having your tooth fixed. Here's the money. God bless!" The young man cried for at least ten minutes. I wanted to crawl under a rock. I started to feel like maybe I had made a huge mistake. Before I was about to walk away, the young man said to me, "Bro, Barry! I received a notice this morning from our school that if I didn't pay $400 today, I would have to leave college. I was several months past due on my payments, and I would have to go back to India with an unfinished degree. This is the exact amount of money I needed to stay at this school!" I was so ecstatic that I could be a part of this tiny miracle!

Another summer, I was asked to travel on behalf of our college to share with other young people how college life was. I enjoyed visiting different places across the country, and I was fortunate enough to meet an incredible young lady named Nicole in a tiny town in North Carolina. She was legitimately everything I ever wanted to find in a girlfriend and a potential wife. It took me several months of attempting to woo her to me via AOL Instant Messenger, but I finally was able to convince her that I was the one for her. We had been dating long-distance for six months and got together to visit my mom for Christmas while we were on break. Nicole was a fresh and mature eighteen, and I was an immature twenty-four. We weren't thinking about the future or where we would be after college when we spent time together. It wasn't something that we discussed. Ever.

I say that because while we were at my mom's house, I had another miraculous event occur. I needed to use the restroom, so I left the living room and walked over to the bathroom. I didn't have a care in the world as I walked into the bathroom. While washing my hands to leave, I felt a strong impression that I was supposed to ask Nicole to marry me. Keep in mind, we hadn't discussed being married; we were only dating for six months, and we were in our first year in college. It didn't make any sense! I started to leave and stopped to pray. I got up and began to leave the bathroom again, and I turned around to pray again. I was legit freaking out! I still couldn't shake the strong feeling that I was supposed to go and ask Nicole to marry me. What I didn't know was that at the very same time, God was speaking to Nicole. She felt this strong impression that I was about to come back and ask her to marry me. She felt like God was telling her that everything would be okay, and that she should say yes! Sure enough, I came into the room, asked her to marry me, and to my great delight, she said yes! I was not prepared to ask her to marry me at all. I didn't have a ring, a watch, a card, flowers or anything. I hadn't asked her parents' permission either. However, at the same time, we both felt the same impression and that this was the right thing to do. I can confidently say that eighteen years later, we are still going strong, and God 100% is a fantastic matchmaker! Yet again, God was faithful to me in a miraculous way.

A couple of years later, I was busy as a real estate agent. I was still preaching at the time, but was supporting my family by selling homes. It was during this period that I had another miracle occur. I had a client who had recently experienced the tragedy of losing her husband. The family was still in so much pain from the loss, and they could not afford the house they were in anymore. They called me to list their home, and we found a buyer very quickly. About three weeks before closing, I woke up around 2:00 a.m. with a powerful impression to pray for this particular client. This wasn't something that happened to me normally. As a matter of fact, I have never had anything like this occur ever again. The impression of praying was so tremendously strong that I was visibly shaking. I prayed for this client for maybe fifteen to twenty minutes and then went to sleep. The next day around 10:00 a.m., I called the client regarding an issue with the closing. At the end of the conversation, I apologetically said, "I had the craziest thing happen last night. I woke up at 2:00 a.m. and felt so strongly that I needed to pray for you." The client seemed off, and said thank you. She quickly rushed off of the phone. So, it was at that moment that I felt like a complete nut job. I was just trying to do the best I could to be obedient to what God was telling me to do. Due to the client's less than enthusiastic response, I wondered if I was losing my mind or had I become a religious weirdo? A couple of days later, this same client called me. She sounded much more awake and more herself this time. She said that she had diabetes and that she had to go to the hospital. I told her that we would keep her in prayer and that everything was back on track for closing. I told her to let me know if she needed anything. I would never forget what she said next: "Well, Barry. You already prayed for me. My heart stopped beating at 2:00 a.m. the other night when you felt led to pray for me. The EMTs were about to call me dead and stopped trying to resuscitate me, but I suddenly came to while you were praying. In a strange turn of events, you were prompted to pray for me the exact few minutes I was lying on the floor with a stopped heart. There was also a shooting nearby, and our family friend passed away that same night. I'm saddened by the loss of my husband and neighbor, but I'm grateful

I was saved from death two nights ago. Thank you for praying for me!"

A few years later, my wife and I were starting to look for a home. Our search took place before the market crashed and homes were selling very quickly and for very high prices. Our budget was low, so it was hard to find anything that worked for us. We had been approved for $135,000. We didn't want a condo or a townhome; we really wanted a large yard so that our dog could run around, and when we had children, they could play. Even for a two bedroom, the homes on the market were selling for $40,000-$60,000 above our max, so we were very close to giving up. We assumed now wasn't the right time to buy and were content renting and waiting it out. After we decided not to stress the buying of a home, I received a call from someone to tell me they had a listing coming on the market soon. They weren't sure what the list price was yet, as they were in the process of doing a CMA, but they recommended I go look at it.

Nicole and I went to go look at the home the next day and were blown away by how nice it was. There wasn't a part of the property that hadn't been renovated. Everything from top to bottom was redone, and the work was done in a way that the person was not planning on leaving soon at all. While at first I was very excited when I saw how large the yard was, I knew we couldn't afford the house. I didn't announce it or try to negotiate with the homeowner. We thanked them for letting us see the home. When we got in the car, I told my wife somberly that we were not going to be able to afford the house. It would be worth at least $180,000.

What happened next is nothing short of incredible. The agent who told me about the home called the seller to discuss the listing value. While the homeowner was listening to the agent, she abruptly stopped the agent, and said, "God told me to sell my home for whatever Barry and Nicole are approved for." She went on to say, "I want to make sure I'm hearing what God is telling me and I'm not missing it, so the way I feel I need to confirm the amount is to tell you what I think they will be approved for. If my number matches their number for what they've been approved for, then I will sell it to them for that price."

The agent began to offer insight that she might not want to do that because she can sell the home for top dollar in this market. The seller insisted again and asked the agent to confirm the number we were approved for. The agent shared that we were approved for $135,000 as our max. The seller began to cry and said that $135,000 was the amount she felt she had heard from God, and would sell us the home for that amount. The agent offered some insight into the market, and said she felt the home would sell for around $185,000. The following day we were told that the seller would sell us the house for $50,000 less than what it was worth. We didn't argue with her! We were overjoyed with the opportunity to move into this fantastic home and raise our first child there.

I started this section of the book with some events where I've personally witnessed God perform some kind of miracle in my life. I knew if I began the entire book this way that it would be hard to digest for most. I do not doubt that God is real and Jesus is the way to Heaven. I don't know these things only because of the preceding stories, I know these things also because of what Jesus did for us, and the story that is told in the Bible. I wanted to share how I've personally seen God move in my life because my testimony is my experience! But, an even more compelling story is that of Jesus in the Bible. Jesus said in John 14:6, "I am the way, the truth, and the life. No one comes to the Father except through me." Jesus didn't offer many paths to God when He said this. Jesus was telling us that He was the only way to Heaven. Jesus was either a liar, a lunatic, or He is the Lord. I choose to believe He is the Lord because He died on the cross for us. Further, I believe Him because the Bible teaches us that He rose from the dead on the third day after death. Jesus proved he was the Lord by overcoming death. The account of Jesus's death, burial, and resurrection is detailed in the New Testament portion of the Bible.

I'm not sure if you're aware of the historicity of the Bible, but historians determine historical facts based on several key factors. While I won't dive deep into how something is determined a historical fact, I do want to mention to you that the Bible is the most well-preserved and historically factual book the world has ever seen. Using key indicators that are used for all other historical facts we believe to be true, things like manuscripts being similar, historical places, key historical figures, and the like all help determine if something can be a historical fact. For example, we can state that a historical fact was that Abraham Lincoln was the president of the United States, and was assassinated. We know this happened due to several historical facts we have collected over time. Reviewing the story of Jesus again with the same critical eye, we know that 2000 years ago a man named Jesus said He was the only way to Heaven. This same man named Jesus then died, and the fact that all of His followers testified to seeing Him alive three days after this death is incredible! The story of Jesus also includes that those same followers were willing to die for what they saw, and this is all a historical fact. We can believe Jesus because the historical facts in the Bible give us the certainty that Jesus said He was the only way to Heaven; He then died and conquered death three days later. This death and resurrection are key because our salvation is based on this event.

I'm going to end this appendix by sharing what many call the "Roman Road to Salvation." The following Bible verses, when put together, show you how to be forgiven for any and all wrong-doing in your life, and have an assurance that you will find hope in Heaven.

We are sinners in need of a Savior.

Romans 3:10, as it is written: "There is no one righteous, not even one."

Romans 3:23 says, "For all have sinned and fall short of the glory of God."

Romans 6:23 says, "For the wages of sin is death, but the gift of God is eternal life in Christ Jesus our Lord."

Jesus took our punishment by dying on the cross for us.

Romans 5:8 says, "But God demonstrates his own love for us in this: While we were still sinners, Christ died for us."

By placing your faith in His work, and making Him the Lord of your life, you will be saved.

Romans 10:13 says, "Everyone who calls on the name of the Lord will be saved."

Outro

Now that you've read through the different chapters in this book, I want to encourage you to grab a list of the actionable takeaways at the end of each chapter and prioritize the items listed there.

Let me be very clear about this: I don't think you need a new list of ideas for your business. Rather than a new list of ideas, you need to execute the ideas you already know are good but you aren't doing. Executing your list of ideas is of the utmost importance, because your competition is more than likely not executing consistently. I've found that most businesses are just treading water and by consistently executing, you will excel.

I remember four to five years ago I began teaching agents my ideas and trade secrets online. Inevitably the sessions would end up on Facebook and YouTube. Agents would many times come to me and ask if I was nervous or concerned about my ideas being shared. I never was concerned about people copying my ideas, because I knew most don't execute at a high level. Things haven't changed! My teaching, scripts, processes, and many other trade secrets are published all over the Internet, but I dare say only a small percentage are able to implement them effectively. Many agents still aren't executing the ideas from the "amazing" conferences they go to year after year.

A key challenge I have had in my business when it comes to execution is just feeling overwhelmed and confused about what the next step is. One resource that has begun teaching me a new way of looking at executing my list of ideas is a new planner I've been using. This resource is called the Evo Planner. Its key selling point is it creates a planner around your personality test results. I happen to have scored that I am an explorer. The to-do list and planning contained in my planner are customized for someone with my personality traits of what the planner calls an explorer.

My version of the planner has a month view, a week view, and a daily view. The planner works as a funnel of sorts. The user decides what they want to see occur in the month ahead and lists the items for the month. As you move into the weekly view, you pull from the list in the monthly view but prioritize it on personal/professional lists. Unsurprisingly, the daily view pulls from the weekly view and it asks you to pick three tasks for the day you want to get done. As simple as this sounds, for me, it has been life-changing. The genius here is taking the large goal and breaking it into smaller digestible pieces.

I have automated a significant list of duties in my business over the last five to six years. To the point that it's one of the things I'm known for across the country in the real estate space. What many agents are surprised to learn is that I don't enjoy setting up automation. It's tedious! It takes a lot of trial and error, patience, and time. While I don't enjoy or have the time for setting up these types of systems, I make time for them by setting apart time every week to tweak things. Little by little over the last five years, I've been able to automate a large portion of my day-to-day. This has enabled my business to scale rapidly, and more importantly, I'm able to focus on things that I am passionate about.

I'm sharing this here because I want you to do the same with the information in this book. Take a few of the Actionable Takeaways at the end of the chapters and jot them down somewhere. More importantly, put that list into your schedule every week and slowly start to make the changes needed to grow your business. You likely won't enjoy it or feel you have time for it, but I guarantee if you begin to fix these aspects of your business little by little, you won't recognize the business a few years from now.

Thank you for reading this book! I truly appreciate you taking the time to grow, and I hope you are able to realize your goals in the near future!

CPSIA information can be obtained
at www.ICGtesting.com
Printed in the USA
BVHW041528201222
654624BV00008B/560